Living the Mysteries

Other books by Robert H. Hopcke

A Guided Tour of the Collected Works of C. G. Jung (Shambhala, 1989)

Jung, Jungians, and Homosexuality (Shambhala, 1989)

Men's Dreams, Men's Healing (Shambhala, 1990)

Same-Sex Love and the Path to Wholeness, edited by Robert H. Hopcke, Karin Lofthus Carrington, and Scott Wirth (Shambhala, 1993)

Persona: Where Sacred Meets Profane (Shambhala, 1995)

There Are No Accidents: Synchronicity and the Stories of Our Lives (Riverhead Books, 1997)

Straight Women, Gay Men: Absolutely Fabulous Friendships, with Laura Rafaty (Wildcat Canyon Press, 2001)

Living the Mysteries

The Spiritual Power of the Rosary
in the Lives of Contemporary People

Robert H. Hopcke

A Crossroad Book
The Crossroad Publishing Company
New York

The Crossroad Publishing Company
481 Eighth Avenue, New York, NY 10001

Printed in the United States of America

This book is set in 11/14 Berkeley Oldstyle. The display fonts are Linoscript and Benguiat Gothic.

Library of Congress Cataloging-in-Publication Data
Hopcke, Robert H., 1958-
   Living the mysteries : the spiritual power of the rosary
in the lives of contemporary people / Robert H. Hopcke.
      p. cm.
   Includes bibliographical references.
   ISBN 0-8245-2104-8 (alk. paper)
   1. Rosary. I. Title.
BX2163.H67 2003
242′.74–dc21
                                        2003008021

1 2 3 4 5 6 7 8 9 10   10 09 08 07 06 05 04 03

In memoriam
Gloria Augusta Hopcke
2001

Ad Jesum per Mariam

Contents

Reading as Praying and Meditating

Tradition is a conversation between the living and the dead. In what they hand down to us, those who have gone before us talk to us of their experience, their way of being, how they have seen God and the world about them. In return, we the living, ideally, listen with openness and respect but also with a responsiveness that comes from our own time and place. Tradition is not a one-way monologue visited by the old and wise onto the young and foolish but rather a dynamic, sometimes impassioned, exchange between generations of family members who love one another. We receive gratefully what is bequeathed, but we must also find a place for what we are given in our own lives.

Like the family silver I just got finished polishing for Christmas, I value the squat, shiny sugar bowl that was my mother-in-law's, the set of serving spoons that were my grandmother's, but in our house we no longer keep these pieces reserved, as they did, for special occasions only. Instead, the sugar bowl and spoons are used everyday, for our coffee in the morning, for our green beans at dinner. Sure, this means these lovely monogrammed pieces tarnish a bit over time (who has time to polish them up more than twice a year!) and perhaps they are even taken a little bit for granted, but in valuing these gifts from the past in our own way, making them a part of our house, we do honor to what we have been given. The dead speak to us in the tradition we are given, but we the living must, with thanks and respect, speak back in our own turn. We must hold up our part and engage in this sacred conversation and keep the dialogue alive, fresh, and new.

The rosary is a rich tradition in Catholicism, and like all traditions, is essentially, I believe, a conversation between the living and dead, between those in heaven and those on earth. As a form of prayer, of course, the rosary is literally a very special kind of conversation: we speak to God through Christ by addressing ourselves to the woman who knew him the most intimately, his mother Mary, and in our contemplation of the mysteries of the rosary, we in our turn listen to what God has to say back to us through the life of his son as experienced by his mother. When we pray the rosary, we speak and we listen.

However, the rosary, as a tradition, is also a conversation in a less literal sense. The use of beads or knotted cord to keep track of prayers is a practice in many religions all over the world, but our rosary finds its origin in the early years of Western monasticism, as a lay person's "psalter" of 150 prayers said in parallel to the formal recitation of the 150 psalms by vowed religious. In the Middle Ages, this venerable form of lay devotion became united with a growing appreciation of the place of the Blessed Mother in her son's work of salvation, and so the rosary was supplemented with specific meditations upon episodes in the life of Christ in which Mary's role was prominent. In this fashion, those who had passed on from this life spoke to their children in faith still on earth, handing on the wisdom of the beads in these prayers and meditations, each age receiving the tradition and speaking back through the rosary. This conversation continues yet today, for example, in the practice of including the Fatima prayer, an innovation to the rosary in the past century and yet, one with profound meaning for contemporary Catholics and others.

I wanted to capture this dynamic and loving conversation about the rosary in this book, and to remain faithful to all the various aspects of this dialogue from the most ethereal to the most concrete. As a psychotherapist and spiritual director, I was eager to hear how the rosary continues to live in the prayer lives of contemporary people—how they came to the rosary or, more frequently, how the rosary came to them, how it changed them or how they in turn changed it. In what ways do the mysteries of the rosary live in the inner lives of contemporary people? How has the rosary led to inner or outer healing, greater intimacy and union with God, a fuller faith, a richer life? How is God, ever ancient and ever new, being seen and felt through the life of Mary and her Son?

Because my own journey of faith has taken me from being a daily rosary-prayer to becoming an actual rosary-maker, my interest is not just in the devotional and spiritual aspect. Through my rosary-making, a craft that dates back thousands of years, I have come to see just how vibrantly the conversation about tradition is being carried forward by those of us who fashion the literal rosaries themselves. The familiar, not to say cliché, plastic, glass, or wood beads on light-weight wirechain—once virtually the only style of rosary in use—has given way in recent years to a stunning and rich palette of forms and materials, as the hearts, minds, and imaginations of Christians bring their devotion to life in the beads: real rose petals, semi-precious gemstones strung on nylon wire, rosaries fashioned out of construction materials and intended as pieces of sculptural art for sacred spaces. The rosary, in this way, has become another kind of conversation; in its aspect as a craft and art form, it is a dialogue between the tangible beauty of the material world—the beads, the centers, the crucifixes, the flowers—and the less tangible world of the soul in contemplation.

By following the mysterious paths in which the Spirit has led me, I have discovered that the rosary, and the devotion to Mary which is its heart, speaks not only to the souls of Roman Catholics, but to men and women of various religious faiths and Christian denominations. The distinctive reverence of the Roman Catholic Church for Mary, of which the rosary is an expression, is indeed that — distinctive — but the living conversation of the rosary tradition has shown me that this reverence is not in any way exclusive. So I was privileged to hear the rosary conversation in the souls of Protestants, those who hold the Blessed Mother in esteem from an unconventionally Christian perspective, even those who claim not to be Christian at all, wholly unchurched and nonpracticing, and yet who hold the rosary and Mary dear to their souls.

I sometimes think of the rosary as a kind of a sacred lasso which, like Peter's dream of a net in Acts, draws into itself a rich and teeming variety of people, a wealth of spiritual experience. We take up our beads, we greet the Blessed Mother and her Son, and behold, in return, she opens her cloak to shelter, protect, sustain, and bless the full welter of all the faithful: prodigal sons, dutiful daughters, those still seeking and knocking and asking, those who have seen and found and touched and believed, the community of saints and the company of sinners. The rosary is indisputably Catholic, but, as I have found in my own life and practice, the rosary is also, and perhaps more importantly, catholic. The rosary includes, accepts, and binds us together into a single family of faith, and through this community, we continue the lively dialogue of tradition with each other and with God.

To make clear all these above reflections, to give tangible form to all of these different layers of the rosary and to continue the conversation of tradition forward in my own way, I was inspired by the Spirit to make this very book you are holding a rosary itself, or as I have put it, a "prosary," a rosary-in-prose. Having made many rosaries from beads over the past years, I was uncertain that it would be possible to make a rosary of a book, but in my questioning, I felt I was in good company. Like Mary after the Annunciation, I, too, asked the Lord, "How can this be?" when the idea for this book, its title and its structure, all came to me as an inspiration in the midst of silent prayer before Office of Readings on the first Monday of Advent at St. Albert's Chapel.

So, I am aware that the form of this book is rather unusual and might therefore be a little confusing for the ordinary reader, especially those for whom the rosary is not second-nature. This book, therefore, is structured as a rosary itself is. We begin with a short section that represents the pendant of a rosary and reflects on the Apostles' Creed and the Lord's Prayer, and then move to the contemplation of what follows: fifteen chapters intended as a meditation upon each of the traditional rosary mysteries. These chapters contain ten smaller selections, stories or reflections, the "beads" of the individual decade, drawn from Scripture, my own reflections and real experiences of the rosary people shared with me personally. The book ends, as the rosary does, with a short section reflecting upon the Salve Regina.

Because I was inspired to try to create a "prosary," my vision of this book is that it will be an instrument of prayer and reflection — not meant to be read in a single sitting cover-to-cover, but instead sampled, savored, picked up, put down, meditated upon. For this reason, I decided not to break the flow of the text in the individual "decade" chapters with names, footnotes, or references as in a conventional book, nor have I added extraneous explanations in these stories about who, what, where, and when the events occurred. Previously published sources are identified in a section of end notes, and all other contributors are acknowledged below, with the exception of those who wished to share their stories in complete anonymity.

So, each little "bead" that follows has its unique place in the "decade" and along the whole string and is meant to be highlighted and enriched in its setting by the stories around it. For some this structure might be a challenge; for some, I hope, it will be an occasion of wonder and contemplation. I would encourage the reader to take up this work the way he or she might take up the rosary: quietly, reflectively and attentively, reading and savoring, holding the selection for a time and turning it over in one's heart and mind, the way one would hold a single bead, before moving on to the next bead, to the next mystery, to the next cycle, letting the natural rhythm of the life of God direct one's soul to what is needful, to what is real, to what nourishes and gives life.

May this book be a new doorway into the rosary tradition. May you find a voice here that helps you to enter into the conversation between the living and dead. May we all, by our attentive listening and faithful response in this conversation, each find our way into the community of saints, to Jesus through Mary.

Entering the Circle

The weight of the silver crucifix is familiar, and its feel always a bit cold at first as I lift it against my forehead and lips to cross myself and begin my prayers. Jesus' body is smooth against my thumb, the edges of the cross complex and ornate — not unlike my faith, sometimes smooth, sometimes jagged, sometimes weighty, sometimes light, sometimes warm, sometimes cold. Still, it is almost always a comfort to hold him in this way, not him, of course, just his image, but I imagine his mother holding him when I hold the crucifix — how small he must have been, how smooth and warm. She felt him as I feel this crucifix, felt him against her forehead, lips, and fingers, and I think of her experience of him as I prepare myself now to pray.

I love the music of the beads. Every rosary has a different voice and timbre, and today I let these small ivory rounds sing out in the silence of the dark chapel, for there is no one else here yet. The sun has not yet risen, and the divine office doesn't begin for another half-hour. Some days, though, I shush them and hold them still, mute and bunched in one hand. They echo so in this small white marble place, and if there are friars trying to pray, I worry that the song of my beads might disturb their lovely deep silence. There is a time to be quiet and a time to sing, and soon we will be singing, I figure, so on those days, I just keep them still. But today, I'm alone, and I let them make their delicate music in the empty air.

Holding that first large bead, I begin with what I believe, what we believe, what we have always believed. *God is the source of everything, the maker of all things visible to our eyes, what we can touch and taste, but really more importantly, the creator of all that is, the invisible, that which we cannot sense, the mystery that surrounds us. This mystery, this invisible creation, is what we, with our heavy words, call heaven: the being around us, in us and through us — not a place but a state, not a perception but a faith.*

Into this creation, out of this profusion, a perfect holiness came to be, in the form of a man, like us in all things except his way of being was not clouded, like ours. He was not deceived by things visible, did not mistake the finite for the infinite, wasn't blind to what he could not sense. He lived in the being of the universe, before his birth, in his human shape, and after his death and resurrection. Indeed, it was for this very reason that this person of God was born of a woman, took full part in this life as we know it: our mortal life, too, is part of God's creation, has its meaning and its purpose. Yet, this man of perfect holiness was so ultimately at one with the spirit of creation, coming directly from its source, that our mere death could not end his life. Once risen, he left us to share in eternal life with the Source of Life Itself whence he came.

I believe we can all share in his spirit. I believe, by grace, we can free ourselves from whatever may impede us, and in this freedom, we can come together in a universal community of love with all those living and all those who have died. In this way, we will not die but will have a new and better life, our body at one with our soul in perfect peace. Amen.

My whispers are a contrast to these momentous pronouncements, and I relish my time to speak of such eternal things so privately and quietly, making this credo a statement of intimacy rather than a public pronouncement in the middle of a Mass, when the single voice of a diverse community bounces off the walls and ceiling of the church. In the morning, here, in the silence of my own soul, over the years, a few of the words have come to serve as punctuation in the rhythm — almighty, earth,

Mary, Pilate, died, heaven, judge, Catholic, saints, sins, life —
and these words become like seams, marking out what joins the
whole cloth of my statement of faith.

I do not wait to invoke Mary three times, the smaller beads
light between my fingers, slipping easily, requiring a bit more attention to hold in my man's hands. Without hesitation, I speak
to her.

*You were and still are his mother. I'm amazed to think what it
would have been like to know him so well and love him so completely – a privilege, a grace, something unique in all history. We
all aspire to accept that divine source of all life into ourselves as you
did, to be transformed as you were, and to become both blessing
and blessed.*

*You are, for us, then also our mother. We ask you, Mother – I ask
you, Mother – be with us all as we stumble through day to day. Let
the way you bore God in your own body and soul show us the way
we, too, can bear God. Help us into life, Mother Mary.*

Today, I wonder today if she ever gets tired of hearing this
from all of us. I talk to her this way every day, the same way,
every day, fifty times a day at least, and sometimes 150 times a
day, and sometimes more than that. What must it be like for her
to hear this over and over and over again from me and from all
of us so constantly? I think of my own mother and all mothers,
the burden of love they carry, the fatigue of it, the exasperation,
the routine of each day of care. Always asking, pulling at the
skirt, looking to be fed, whining and crying, anxious silences,
separations, what now, what next?

I'm on the third bead of the pendant when I recover my attention from this long distraction, and here is the genius of the
rosary: the feel of the fat bead, so abrupt against fingers used
to the littler ones, brings me back to myself, reminds my errant
soul: time to cross myself and move on, letting the beads sing

another bar or two, as I murmur my short sentence of praise: *God is eternal, his son and his spirit also eternal.*

I love the medal in the middle of this particular rosary, this artful spray of miniature roses in gold, the crossroads of these antique ivory strands. Thin and flat, it feels so insubstantial against the tip of my index finger, and yet, when I let the beads hang off my finger, what is clear is that this small medal is indeed the center: the whole weight of the rosary hangs upon these three tiny corners. So each time I come to the first mystery, I come to this center, this doorway into the cycle of meditation for the day.

Mother of God, she is the Gate of Heaven. She is for us humans the beginning of the Beginning, the center of the Center. But this center is likewise the end, for here, my fingers find the completion of their journey around this circle of beads, the place where speech stops, the start of the eternal silence which is of course the true goal of contemplation. So, when I set out from this center on my pilgrimage, the tips of my fingers anticipate the end far away, the time and the place when no more can be said, the finality to be found also at the center.

The Joyful
Mysteries

Annunciation

*And the angel said to her, "Do not be afraid, Mary, for you
have found favor with God. . . . The Holy Spirit will come upon
you and the power of the Most High will overshadow you;
therefore, the child to be born will be called holy."*

(Luke 1:30, 35)

Hail, Mary . . .

Joyous mysteries today, five episodes of anticipation and hope:
it is Monday and a new week begins. Mary hears for the first
time that she will bear a child, and my mind's eye delights in
seeing her, all those hundreds and hundreds of annunciations
I have seen in my life having left their indelible marks on my
imagination. The graceful curve of her body, bending to receive
God, yet still standing in her place, crowded by the flurrying
robes of Gabriel and the brilliant light all around her, a profuse
providence raining down upon her, coursing through her.

In the stained glass window at my parish depicting this
scene, the artist has crammed the pane full of flowers. All the
cornices, all the pieces of furniture, all the clothing in the scene
are rife with floral motifs, as if the power of God's creative force
is manifesting itself in everything as Mary hears the news.

So today, this image of abundance comes to me, as I use Jesus'
own prayer. Its familiarity is a ballast, the touchstone, the home
base of the daily rosary journey.

You are holy, my God, my Father. Come into creation fully. Make us one with you. You have always provided for our needs. Provide for them today again. Protect us from our own weakness and from the ill will of others by helping us always remember that what is true and right is the source of real power and peace. Amen.

The waves of the Aves lap at my soul, and the beads slip one by one past my fingertips. I sit on the beach of this contemplative sea and listen to the sound of these waves, my inner self pondering the mystery of the Annunciation, thinking of Phil waiting for news of whether he has passed his licensing exam, wondering about my own application for a study grant in Italy and whether or not it will bear fruit, praying actively for spiritual and emotional renewal for the more discouraged and stuck clients in my psychotherapy practice.

To receive renewal requires openness, and around the fourth bead I remember that to receive God requires humility. I'm not a very humble person, so I spend three beads recalling times in the past day when I missed the opportunity to be more self-effacing, less visible, when I took the opportunity to gratuitously display and assert myself. *Hail, Mary, help me envision what it might have been like to have not said anything, to have accepted the traffic jam, the slow waitress, the lack of response, to let such things move past me and through me. You are transparent in that window: help me to be transparent, to step aside, to wear myself lightly enough to allow the sunlight of God's all-encompassing love to shine through me to others. Help me to be open to bearing God.*

full of grace . . .

Making a rosary is like composing a piece of music. Each rosary has its own "key," so to speak, an overall look or tone. Some can be kind of modern and angular, with spare cross, simple

22

centers, clear beads. Some can be antique, redolent of the nine-teenth century or even older, perhaps heavy, dark and medieval. The possibilities are endless, of course, and the parts have a lot to do with this "key," but the fact is, each rosary has its own particular character. When I am making a rosary, everything I choose—the beads, the wire, the spacers—all need to be in that particular, individual key or the rosary looks "off." It can be a mysterious thing, this process of composition. I don't really know myself how it happens, except to say it's through sheer inspiration and by maintaining my sense of balance and good taste. Are those aspects of the Spirit at work?

the Lord is with you.

Then that lovely interior silence happens, and I feel my soul gently lift upward — by the seventh or eighth bead I am lulled into forgetting myself, permitting the prayers to say themselves as I float above, both consciousness and unself-consciousness, two different notes in a single beautiful chord of experience. I spend some time there, or so it feels to me, long moments sus-pended. How long? Perhaps a minute, perhaps twenty. All that exists is the awareness, the prayer praying themselves as I look down from above. I am there praying, but I am also not there. I am beyond there. My soul moves into the dark and wonderful si-lence, and I listen to what I was from a brief experience of what I shall sometime be. May God grant it to me. Long moments. I do not know how long.

I only return when I feel the large bead nudge my thumb, open my eyes, see the friars who have joined me, watch the lights of the chapel grow bright and buzz, hear the pages flip-ping. All that time, I have been praying the Annunciation, hardly begun. I take a deep breath, rub my fingers over the smooth, cool ivory, and with a blink, resolve to finish the rosary after morning prayer. Till then, Mother. I cross myself, slip the beads over my head and into my shirt, and bend over to retrieve the gray psalter.

Blessed are you among women . . .

So many of the conventional pious representations of the Annunciation do not really get at the real mystery of this story, the spiritual truth that I meditate upon. For me, it makes sense, in a way, to start the whole rosary with this particular mystery, as God shows forth his wonder through life situations that seem at first to oppose our expectations and the accepted mores of the society around us.

I don't know how many people see all those beautiful annunciations which adorn our churches and museums and really look at Mary's face. Most of the time it looks to me as though she is just plain terrified. Seeing an angel, wings unfurled, speaking to her in her own room would be enough to frighten most fourteen-year-old girls anyway, but then, in her time and culture, to be told that through no sinful action of her own she is pregnant out of wedlock and that she is to do nothing to end this pregnancy, that is, it is God's will—as I say the rosary, I put myself in her situation and let the implications of this sink in to me, as if I were her. Social ostracism, shame brought down upon her whole family, a wonderful relationship with her prospective husband forever ruined, a marriage never to be, no proper upbringing for her child, living hand-to-mouth on the charity of relatives, a life of misery really in a culture in which women were hardly seen as human and in which their sexual impropriety merited severe religious and social condemnation.

Really, who would believe her, even now in our own day and time, if she said publicly, "How can this be, since I have not been with a man?" Is there any of us who would not simply presume she was lying to avoid the consequences of her lack of sexual control, her irresponsibility, her sinfulness? I'm old enough to remember a time when such a pregnancy was the cause of intense social disapproval, and even today, within supposedly Christian circles, it isn't hard to find people who would cluck and snort and declare her guilty of sexual sin, wave church teaching and conventional morality in her face and turn away from her, without offering to help her or her baby, without a thought to the way that the mystery of the Annunciation confronts and ultimately condemns, not Mary, but rather our own religious self-righteousness.

God comes into the world through situations that scandalize, that overturn conventional morality, that dare us to see past simplistic notions of sanctity. What is a mystery here is that sometimes what we have been told by our culture, and even by religious authorities, does not limit God's action. After all, it was the holiest and most righteous of religious authorities in Mary's own time that would have supported Joseph's summary rejection of her, her banishment and condemnation.

and blessed is the fruit of your womb, Jesus.

When I meditate upon the Annunication, I feel so much solidarity with Mary. I experience being gay in the way that I imagine she experienced her pregnancy. I didn't ask for it. I did nothing that caused it. If you put it in the fairy-tale terms of the Bible story, it is very much as if the angel of the Lord came down and said, "Poof, you are gay." To which I say back, "But how can this be? I was raised to be heterosexual. I dated a woman in high school." And the angel says back to me, "God wants it this way." And there I am, thinking ahead about what that means for me: I am going to be roundly denounced by all religious authorities, declared sick by psychological professionals, rejected by some family and friends, misunderstood and pitied by others, made to feel unwelcome, unloved, and unlovable in most places in my society—all of which, of course, will be justified by blaming me for what has happened. No question of anyone taking some time perhaps to meditate upon the way that my homosexuality might have come upon me as Mary's pregnancy did—through the mysterious action of the Holy Spirit who wished to manifest God's consciousness in the flesh. No, instead of seeing my sexual orientation as God's mysterious, miraculous, ironic way of humbling the proud and lifting up the lowly, I am going to be dismissed as a sinner, viewed with suspicion. All my attempts to claim my homosexuality as gift, as sacred, as a way Christ is made flesh through love—these, too, will be dismissed. Let's just say that, when I meditate upon the reality of the Annunciation as it probably actually was in the life of that young woman in Palestine, I understand where she is coming from and what she is facing.

That's why I ask her for help—help in bearing the sneering, the indignity of unjustified condemnation, the lack of compassion, the strictures of conventional morality. She folds her hands, bows, and accepts that this is indeed God's will for her life—not out of masochism or self-hatred. Oh no, she accepts herself and what she is because of a deep trust in God's action in the world, the spark of Christ hidden, for now, within her own body. It is a wonderful thing to walk about with this kind of consciousness about my homosexuality, to contemplate the possibility that, like Mary, I am bringing a very unexpected form of salvation into the world in an incarnate way—scandalous, unacceptable, transformative of every social expectation and religious dogma. That is the mystery of the Annunciation to me—that Jesus comes to us in such an unexpected way—and with each bead I pray for someone who needs the Blessed Mother's help to accept and live this mystery.

Holy Mary, Mother of God . . .

When I took up rosary-making, I didn't expect that the actual rosary-making itself would become a spiritual practice, but it has for me, and this unexpected grace is one I would dare to say visits most rosary-makers. That's why we rosary-makers are so darned enthusiastic, why we find ourselves so thoroughly absorbed into the craft (if we have the time, energy, and money, that is!). I was blind-sided by how much spiritual growth would come for me, not just from the praying, but from the actual making of the rosaries. So I'm happy to go into detail about the way rosary-making has been a part of my soul's growth and has taught me lessons I'd have never learned otherwise.

Such as patience. I'm not known for my patience, but there is something so peaceful about making rosaries. I move into a whole different rhythm which, over the years, has helped me to grow greatly in my capacity to be calm in the face of difficulties. The blessings I have received from rosary-making almost outnumber those received from praying the rosary.

Putting together a rosary is a process that cannot be rushed. I always make sure I set aside an hour or two, take a moment or two to pray and get in the right frame of mind, and then just let what happens happen. Each one is new and different. I learn something new with each one, inside and out. So, they are a little bit like children – unique, beautiful, unexpected, delightful, but of course at times frustrating, too.

There are days I wake up and it comes to me, "Yup, today is going to be a rosary day," and so it is. I just sit in long hours of silence at my craft table, looking out on the garden, thinking things over, praying a little, giving thanks as each set of beads comes together, loving the colors, the shapes, the feel of the stones, remembering other rosaries I've made, letting images of rosaries I have yet to make slowly come to mind in response to certain materials I'm working with. And before I know it, a whole day has gone by in my own private contemplative retreat with my dishtowel in front of me to keep the beads rolling off the table, my stacks of trays with all the parts organized, my spools of wire, my shears and pliers.

My parish has a rosary-making group, but I'm ashamed to say that I've never gone. I'm not interested in knotting cord or chaining together rosary kits for the missions or postabortion ministries or Catholic relief services. I have sent some of my rosaries to those places but privately. The group thing, for some reason, doesn't appeal to me. My rosary-making is like my prayer, just me and God.

pray for us sinners now . . .

The rosary came to me in the midst of a terrible period of my life. My work life as an artist was successful beyond what I could have imagined after many long years of plugging away, but commercial success brought with it a very dark shadow. I didn't expect that part of it. I found myself right in the "belly of the beast" — the thoughtless, insensitive, hurly-burly of capitalism as practiced in this country. As an artist, I found the whole commercial world almost stupendous in its obtuseness: rather than see the beauty of my work, appreciate the symbolism, take in the images as I intended, as ways of enlarging the soul, refining the spirit, lifting and challenging the mind to new ways of seeing and feeling, I found myself in interminable conversations with agents and merchants about prices, discounts, contracts — always money, money, money. Lots of lip-service to the art, lots of patronizing looks and comments to me when I would protest or ask to be treated differently.

Basically, I was very successful but always enraged. My friends, especially my partner, would try to tell me this tactfully, but I didn't really see it. When I look back on those years, I remember just perseverating about what made me angry, chewing on it over and over and over—every little slight, every sign of disrespect, every wrangle over this, that, or the other. It's embarrassing to admit but sometimes I would actually go on walks just in order to rehearse in my mind what, day by day, I was furious about. As a misguided way to hang on to my own sanity and viewpoint in the midst of a world of subjective opinions, reviews, picks, and pans that comes along with commercial success and wide public attention, I began to keep a written list of things that I was furious about, things I resented, things that made me angry.

All this probably would have been bad enough for my own mental health—and indeed it was, as I came down with all sorts of stress-related physical symptoms during that period — but when I now look back, I can see how I was one of the more difficult people I knew. I could get away with some of this diva behavior, since, being an artist, people expect you to be a little kooky and temperamental. And also, while giving myself full permission to vent my rage, anger, frustration, and resentment, my good sense of humor made some of my rants wickedly entertaining. But I often dropped the veneer of humor and then my expressions of rage would become, in the unforgettable word of a friend of mine, "ugly."

Into this emotional climate and downward spiral of wrath, the rosary re-entered my life. I had never been especially devoted to the practice, but having lived in Italy for a year as part of my art training, I had warm associations to the rosary. I used to wait for the bus home after class by ducking into a small oratorio in the late afternoon just before Mass, mostly to keep warm, and I'd listen to the rhythmic murmuring and clicking of a few little old ladies in black wool and lace mantillas saying the prayers. The church was lit only by candles, and the quiet, gentle sound of "Hail Marys" was so soothing. After a few weeks of just listening, I realized I had learned all the prayers — in Italian.

Many years later, in the midst of this dark time of success, my partner's sister, as a kind of campy joke, sent me out their mother's rosaries after her death — along with her turbans and scarves, thinking, I imagine, that I might be able to use these various articles when doing drag at Halloween or something. To tell you the truth, I don't really know what Debbie was thinking, but when I saw those two cheap plastic rosaries, I can honestly say that the last thing on my mind was that contemplative prayer would be a way out of my rage and depression. I took up the beads that first day as an admittedly lame way to honor the memory of my partner's mother, who had been very good to me — that was really my conscious purpose. My positive associations to these prayers paved the way to my committing now to pray the rosary each day for the coming month, which is what I did.

Once I began to pray the rosary, however, suddenly I found that all my rageful ruminations were being brought into an orderly structure. What I had been doing on my walks and in my lists freestyle, so to speak — muttering about who I hated, chewing on grudges — I was now doing for fifteen solid minutes beneath my regular recitation of *Ave Marias* and *Padre Nostros*. Truth to tell, I was meditating very little on Mary and Jesus. I spent more time on how I had been done wrong, how unfairly and disrespectfully I was being treated, how pitiful it was that here I was doing better than ever and hating it. Not exactly the most inspiring meditations — endless interior complaints about how nothing was good enough for me and my inflated sense of self. But the minor miracle of the rosary was this: at the end of those fifteen minutes of half-assed prayer, if you even want to call it that, I was no longer angry. Before the rosary, all my interior wounds, all my furious self-pity, would just keep bleeding inside me throughout the day. After the rosary, my mind was quiet, my body relaxed. I felt purged, clean, at peace, and because I felt better, I behaved better toward others: no need to bark at anyone, no reason to vent my spleen on innocent bystanders and loved ones.

The important gift the rosary taught me was the inner and outer mechanics of emotional containment, a contemplative detachment that naturally occurred as the prayers lifted me out of my everyday consciousness and gave a higher perspective, a "God's-eye view." As the rosary became a regular, available outlet for me, frankly, to bitch about what was wrong with my life, those around me received a grace as well. They were relieved from the necessity of having to hear me. So, the rosary was a sort of divine psychotherapy. You go to a therapist only when your friends can't stand hearing about your problems anymore. I went to Mary, and whether she wanted to hear me grind on and on, I don't know. But I had the sense someone was listening, and in the end, I'd put away my beads consistently feeling healed of my distress.

The rosary continues to be a part of my everyday life. Circumstances gradually changed in my life, nothing dramatic, just a slow, steady shift. Little by little, the commercial art world lost my interest. I, in my turn, decided to withdraw from such close contact with those circles; first in small ways, and then in larger ways, I began to go in another direction. Bead by bead I walked away.

Sometimes I trip on the shape of it and think it's like a little lasso, reining in my egotism and its gazillion manifestations, keeping me in one place, contained and held, long enough for the storm to pass, long enough for me to have an experience of something different, something bigger, something deeper.

Think of the encircling arms of a patient mother holding a bratty child in a tantrum. There is a lot of symbolism in it.

But one truth remains: how I feel at the end of fifteen decades is never how I felt when I started.

and at the hour of our death.

I have been given life. That's the announcement to me. I realize I do not hold the incarnation of God's word within me as Mary did, but in a certain sense I do, or I could. Maybe this mystery is asking me to follow Mary's example, to say to myself and to God, "Be it done unto me according to thy word." But *what*, let *what* be done unto me? Well…everything. This mystery asks me to embrace all the events in my life, and it is the Word within me, that tiny divine spark, that lets me say, as Mary did, "Yes, I will grow through everything I do, everything I say, everything I think, everything I experience."

Amen.

Second Joyful Mystery

Visitation

Blessed are you among women, and blessed is the fruit of your womb! And why is this granted to me, that the mother of my Lord should come to me? For behold, when the voice of your greeting came to my ears, the babe in my womb leaped for joy! And blessed is she who believe that there would be a fulfilment of what was spoken to her from the Lord. (Luke 1:42-45)

Hail, Mary...

I don't know why it is, when I say the rosary in the morning, I find all my prayers are usually intercessory. I could be reviewing my day to come and asking for various things for myself, but usually I do that at Mass. Instead, I have noticed that my morning rosaries are always for other people and their needs. And the rosary mystery I associate most closely with this intercessory prayer for others is the Visitation.

Mary stayed with her cousin Elizabeth for months, so I have no doubt that she was busy doing all the housework, laundry, sweeping, cleaning, cooking—pouring herself out for her aged, pregnant cousin. So I keep all that service of hers in mind when I pray, asking God to help, sustain, and inspire all forms of helpers: housecleaners, gardeners, counselors, social workers, telephone operators. Do we really realize how much we depend on others for even the simplest things? Bus drivers, truckers, all the people in the field picking the vegetables and fruit we eat—none of us would have anything on the table if it weren't for their service. Who remembers them and the dangers they have put themselves into for us? And for that matter, policemen, firemen, rescue workers, military personnel. They, too, are serving. They, too, are spending their lives so that others might be safe, healthy, at peace.

The mystery of the Visitation is the helper mystery, a time for me to draw back and look at our interdependence, the way each of us is strung together with everyone else, like the rosary I am holding. In Mary's time, things were so simple and life so hard that this dependence on others was a daily reality. But nowadays things are so complex, and so much of what makes our life possible is invisible to us, happening behind the scenes. I use the rosary to pray for those who help me day to day, people I don't even know. It is a good mystery for counting the blessings of providence, one by one, as the hymn goes, the humble blessings of my life, and to pour myself out in prayer for those who have been providential, for their safety, for their wholeness, for their health.

full of grace . . .

When I began praying the rosary, it was because we were assigned to do so every night for a month as part of our religion class at Catholic school. At first, the thought of it was slightly overwhelming and seemed just way too time-consuming to me, really almost a waste of time. But then, I thought about all those people who needed prayers, people who could really use a miracle, and so, I did as I was told.

To be honest, praying a decade of the rosary, just one decade, seemed like a chore at first to me as a teenager, and, for my good intentions, I can't say I really kept any of them in my mind, although they were always in my heart. Not until the fourth or fifth day, after I had begun in earnest, did I begin to feel the real effect of the prayer, when praying a decade had become routine enough so I could actually think about those people who needed a miracle.

That was when my prayer felt different. The words weren't just coming out of my mouth any more. Instead, it felt as if the words of the rosary went from my head, through my heart, and then out of my mouth, ready to be captured by those for whom my prayers were intended. In this way, the rosary has become a part of my life, not just words, and I have come to feel the immense power of prayer which is certainly in all of us.

the Lord is with you.

I took a box of rosaries to a soccer game — just to do a double check before I sent them out, and I couldn't believe how all the children were drawn to them. One little boy asked in particular for a "Christmas" rosary, by which he meant the pretty gold rosaries I make with green and red beads. When he got his Christmas rosary, he was so happy. He must have smiled for ten minutes, and he showed his father and all his friends. Another little girl just had to have one too. She wasn't Catholic, but I gave her one anyway — she was so insistent! I happen to know that she comes from a very troubled family, where lots of foul language and humiliation are the norm. So I like to think she was so attracted to the rosary because she could feel the loving presence in it.

On the other side of the age range, my aunt is a rosary-maker and she gives her rosaries away, mostly to her senior citizen friends shut away in nursing homes and care facilities with no real worldly possessions. They find great comfort in the rosaries made for them, holding them, praying on the beads.

They don't have to send them away to the laundry. They can lay their various rosaries and beads on their beds for others to admire, because the rosary is one of the only possessions they are allowed to have with them at all times. It might seem such a small thing to many of us, but I would very much like people to know the wonderful feeling rosaries give to the elderly.

Blessed are you among women . . .

I'm continually struck by how modest people tend to be about the place of the rosary in their lives, perhaps even shy. At Rich's Christmas party, Carol and I had a chance to really sit down and chat for once, instead of marching in parades or talking a bit before Mass. Since her father and my mother both died on the same day in the past year, we ended up talking about how we both realized that the anniversary of their deaths is actually going to be on Good Friday in the coming year, a bittersweet observance. She told me that his birthday next Wednesday, right in the middle of the Christmas season, also eclipses the way she might like to memorialize him. "With all the flowers and everything in the church already, you know," she said. A few moments later, when I told her that I was collecting rosary stories for a book on the place of the rosary in people's lives, she said, "Well, this really isn't a story, just kind of little tidbit, but when my father was facing his operation last year, knowing that there really wasn't any choice, he would have to be operated upon, but also knowing that he might not wake up, that it was very possible he might die on the table, I went home to be with him, and I took him a rosary. Now my partner, Joanna, had an aunt who had been to Rome, where she had gotten this rosary that had been blessed by the pope. She gave it to Joanna, who gave it to me to give to my father.

"And you have to understand, my parents have a very deep, almost childlike kind of faith, so hearing that this rosary had been blessed by the pope himself meant a lot. My dad said that before he went in for the operation, praying with that rosary brought him a great deal of peace around what was to come. So after he died, we made sure he had it with him in the casket, but my mother asked me to get it for her before the burial because she said that she wanted it to be with her when it was her time. I have to say, that rosary meant a lot to me, too, just knowing the journey it had traveled, from Rome, to my partner, to my father and now to my mother, to bring peace in a difficult time of our lives, bringing Joanna and me into the family in a special way."

"Mary loves all her children," I said to her. "I want to make sure people hear that in the stories. And your story makes me think that it actually is the way one of the older, and wiser, rosary-makers I know says it is: each rosary we make is destined for the hands of a particular individual, for a particular grace."

Carol smiled. "That's interesting. I know that rosary had quite a journey to get into my father's hands."

"And the journey isn't over yet," I told her, thinking of her mother, my father, coping with the holidays, their grief, the full life they each had with their spouse.

"No, it isn't, is it? These things are so profound sometimes."

and blessed is the fruit of your womb, Jesus.

My own parish doesn't really say the rosary at all, and I miss that aspect of spirituality. My job requires that I travel a great deal, and since I always try to keep up my daily Mass attendance, I have the chance to visit a lot of different parishes and places. Almost every one of them says the rosary before or after Mass, and sometimes it's a really big group of people. My impression is with younger Catholics in our parish; they think rosary beads are just for old ladies, something from another time and place, probably because our parish really doesn't do very much officially to promote or teach the rosary as a prayer. So I'm always a little taken aback in the places I visit to see the whole church filled with people, all kinds of people, young, old, men, women, saying the rosary before Mass. I go home and I want to say, "You know, in other churches, the rosary is a way the whole parish prays together. It's not just for little old ladies."

Saying the rosary together before Mass creates a whole different kind of spirit in the church. Rather than chatting and running around, people come into church, they hear the rosary and they really can't help but join in — not with a couple of dozen people saying the prayers together and the whole space full of "Hail Marys." Some of us relics remember the time before the Vatican II changes, when everything was silent and reverent in church. You'd never sit and chit-chat before Mass. There was a holiness that people respected and took the time to create. Saying a communal rosary before Mass is, I've noticed, a way to create that reverence, without being heavy-handed. Are there any Catholics that don't have a deep affection for the "Hail Mary"? If there are, I haven't met them.

Another thing I've noticed in my travels is that the rosary generates community feeling. The Mass then begins with people already having a sense of being with each other, something I really appreciate, especially when I am not at home. I know I can walk into the church, sit down and right away, I'm praying with these people. The rosary makes me feel right at home.

Holy Mary . . .

Echo of his life
Radiant Child
of the God of Light

Born without stain
Yet you remain one of us
The one whom sin has not touched.

O Immaculate One
Shrine holding God's son
We fear not to approach you
In your sublimity
For you are, O Mary,
shining humility.

Mother of God . . .

Another aspect of a religious tradition, though, is most certainly its particularity. I've found in my rosary-making that the rosary is unusual, because prayer beads reach across time and tradition. The Roman Catholic rosary finds its natural cousin in the Buddhist *mala,* and the Greek Orthodox *choktis.* Father Thomas Keating, Trappist contemplative and internationally known teacher of Centering Prayer, is fond of quoting the verse from Psalm 42, "Deep is calling on deep in the roar of the waters," as a poetic way to say that all contemplative traditions meet each other at a point beneath the individual perspectives and boundaries. I have found this to be true with prayer beads. My love for the rosary and my intimacy with its feel, its forms, its strength, its symbolism awakens me when a friend of mine brings forward his beautiful red-and-gold Eastern prayer rope with its intricate knots making crosses that my fingers just want to touch, its feather-light fringe spilling over my knuckles like holy water.

Being in California, I've come across so many beautiful Buddhist prayer beads at craft fairs and other gatherings, and it's been all I could do sometimes to refrain from buying some of these unusual beads, so perfectly carved from types of wood rarely seen in the stores I frequent. I cannot help thinking how lovely they would look with this center or this cross, how easy it would be to take them apart to be restrung into rosaries. And yet I have not dared to do so.

Why not? Is it merely vacuous multiculturalism that has stayed my hand and my checkbook, a political correctness that yaks at me inwardly about spiritual disrespect to the beads and to the craftsperson? Or is it rather a kind of tact born of my awareness that personally I would very much dislike a lovely wooden rosary I had strung to be harvested like so much inanimate stuff, bought simply to be snipped apart and pieced together, plied into unwilling use in a fashion and a religious tradition not originally intended.

In pondering the issue here of whether a bead is a bead is bead, I admit no such scruples about necklaces and bracelets I've come across here and there at flea markets and curio shops. But their makers did not fashion these items for a spiritual, religious, or contemplative purpose, but rather for mere ornamentation. So to disassemble a piece of ordinary jewelry and to refashion it into an object for contemplative prayer instead gives me a bit of thrill, whereas the idea of buying a *mala* for no other reason than to get my hands on ninety-nine beautiful beads for a couple of rosaries goes against the grain of my feeling. No one would know, of course, but I would. And so would the original Creator.

pray for us sinners now . . .

I wake gently, spontaneously, fully rested after three days of silent retreat, and before I leave my bed to find my way about my dark room, I do what I came here to El Retiro to do for this week: I lie still and collect myself. I can hear nothing beyond the light curtains by my head except the occasional sound of a bird, and after a few moments of meditation, I rise, and the tug at my fingertips reminds me. I fell asleep with my rosary in hand and I hope I am not too late. It seems not; out the window I peek and see just a dark blue night and a few tiny stars. Feeling about like a blind man, I find the wide cup and down the mouthful of cold coffee left over from yesterday, pull on my clothes, and greet the not-yet-dawn with a long, slow, deep breath, the little bouquet of crystal still warm in my hand.

I make my way down the path, past the chapel, past the roses, past the fountain, past St. Joseph, and step into the meeting room. A small, savory pleasure it is to be where the doors are never locked. I feel gratitude. Bowed out like the prow of a ship over the hillside, the room is round with wide high windows, and beyond it, the balcony is, as usual, deserted. The sky is empty but the violet over the distant hills is lined in deep red, turning orange with every passing minute. Planes angle up from my right, gliding and circling through the air without a sound, and I watch them come and go as I might watch snowflakes or raindrops.

I begin my rosary, making the sign of the cross, a wordless silent rosary before the promise of the impending dawn and the demands of the coming day. Soon the light, the heat, the shadows, the life of the day will be with us, and I incline my head and my heart to begin my prayer.

Out of the corner of my eye, I see a small movement. Without turning my head, but rather just allowing my vision to expand, I catch a glimpse of a fellow retreatant, another early riser, across the balcony, sitting very still. Who he is, I do not know. We will not be speaking, but together in prayer we face the east, lined bright along the ridge tops with a sun we haven't yet seen.

41

and at the hour of our death.

God has done great things for me. He has given me the power to do things that I would normally fear doing. I asked him for help and he granted it to me.

God has done great things for me. When I am lonely, God comes to me and gives me the company I need to get through difficult times. I asked for help and he granted it to me.

God has done great things for me. When I feel lost and have no one to turn to, he stands by me and leads me in the right direction. I asked for help and he granted it to me.

God has done great things for me. When I am angry at the world, God comforts me with the power of his Holy Spirit. I asked for help and he granted it to me.

God has done great things for me. When I am jealous, God comes to me and makes me realize what gifts I have to treasure. I asked for help and he granted it to me.

God has done great things for me. When life is difficult, and you need an everlasting friend, turn to him. Ask for help. He *always* granted it to me.

Amen.

Third Joyful Mystery

Nativity

The time came for her to be delivered. And she gave birth to her first-born son and wrapped him in swaddling cloths, and laid him in a manger, because there was no place for them in the inn. And in that region there were shepherds out in the field keeping watch over their flock by night. And an angel of the Lord appeared to them.... And the angel said to them, "Be not afraid; for behold I bring you good news of a great joy which will come to all the people; for to you is born this day in the city of David a Savior, who is Christ the Lord." ...When the angels went away from them into heaven, the shepherds said to one another, "Let us go over to Bethlehem and see this thing that has happened, which the Lord has made known to us." (Luke 2:6–11; 15)

Hail, Mary...

I'm always impressed with how much spiritual wisdom resides in tradition. There is no doubt about the capital-W wisdom that lives in the capital-T tradition for me, but certain aspects of the rosary bring forward to my awareness how much even in the smaller, homier little-t traditions of folk piety and customs, God's nature can be revealed and illuminated.

I sit here at noon on Thursday, and it is time to join the Dominican brothers in their corporate rosary. We are neatly lined

43

up on either side of the chapel in our old-style monastic choir stalls, some kneeling, some geezers like me, sitting with rosaries in hand, the silence gathering at the time to begin draws near. Since the wall-to-wall marble here at St. Albert's makes for astonishing acoustics in this jewelbox of a chapel, I can hear with perfect clarity the echoes of the friars' lunch being prepared over in the refectory — banging pans, conversations, a door opening and closing a couple of times. Moreover, I am fresh from a morning of somewhat difficult psychotherapy sessions with people in pain who, of course, can be argumentative, intellectualizing, demanding.

In short, I arrive here for the rosary and I am distracted, so distracted in fact that I go all through the familiar motions, crossing myself, mouthing the prayers, counting the beads draped over my index finger, when suddenly the fog of preoccupation clears and I hear Brother Robert announce, "The third Joyful Mystery, the Nativity of our Lord,"

I think, "Oops, where was I? Seem to have missed the first two." I check where I am on my set of beads and there I am, smack in the middle. Comforted slightly to know that at least my hands have been praying, even if my mind and heart have not followed suit, I then realize, "Joyful mysteries? Oh right, it's Thursday. Joyful? I don't feel joyful." Where have I been?

How artificial it suddenly seems to me in that moment to cycle through these sets of mysteries according to the day of the week: joyful Monday and Thursday, sorrowful Tuesday and Friday; glorious Wednesday and Saturday. Who feels joyful on Thursday, the bulk of the work week pressing firmly on the soul? What about all that "thank God for Friday" energy we have to put aside to contemplate Christ's passion, whether we feel like it or not? And is there anything more inglorious than "hump-day" Wednesday, neither here nor there?

Yet my fingers walk down the path of beads, and slowly, as has happened so many times for me, I begin to appreciate the challenge of this devotion. We are contemplating the Nativity — regardless of how we feel in this moment, regardless of what has happened before, regardless of what will happen after. Take a moment, the blue agates in my hand whisper invitingly. Take a moment, they say, and steal away to Jesus. Leave aside the pots and pans. Let the morning be what it was. Is it possible that Christ is being born right now, in this moment? How is that possible? Meditate on this mystery, the beads suggest, follow the brothers around you and meditate a little.

Is Christ being born right now in the same fashion he was born then — in an unexpected place and time? Could he be born right now in the midst of the pain and resistance of my clients, in my own questions about my compassion, my patience, my skill, in my fatigue and in my hope about my work? Are these the poor and unlikely mangers where I might, like Mary, Joseph, and the shepherds, find the newness of God being born for me?

Consider this improbability, if you wish to know God. That is the inviting wisdom of saying a rosary of joyful mysteries on a less-than-joyful, work-a-day Thursday. See past the present with its trials and tribulations, its boredom and busyness. Contemplate the eternal birth of the Word made flesh, dwelling among us. Perhaps the pain of those I encounter in my work and my own unsureness of the outcome of our healing are the birth pangs that Mary felt, something new and still immature coming into being, a divine consciousness that appears to our own distracted and unseeing mortal eyes as nothing more than a tiny baby for now, brought forth wailing amid darkness and poverty.

So improbable a cause for joy, this baffling nativity of God among us. As improbable — and as potentially awesome — as Thursday.

full of grace . . .

When I was first contacted to make a Mexican wedding rosary via e-mail through my rosary website, I managed not to show my ignorance about what a Mexican wedding rosary was. At first, I thought the young woman who had written me was talking about what is known as a "ladder rosary," which I did know was a style of rosary found in Mexico, in which the beads are strung horizontally one by one between two parallel chains, creating a ladder effect, rather than being strung from end to end the way most rosaries are. But unsure of myself, I consulted a few of my rosary-making elders and uncovered a lovely tradition.

"During a Mexican wedding ceremony, a *lazo* (lasso), or large rosary, is draped around the bride and groom while they are kneeling at the altar. Padrinos, two special relatives the couple has chosen as additional 'sponsors' of their wedding (in addition to their parents of course) may also present them with coins (for prosperity), a Bible and a rosary during the ceremony. After the ceremony, lucky red beads are sometimes tossed at newlyweds. And a beautiful reception tradition has all the guests during the couple's first or last dance create a heart shaped circle around them.

"As part of the ceremony to symbolize unity, a large loop of rosary beads or a lasso (cord) is placed in a figure-eight shape around the necks of the couple after they have exchanged their vows. It also is beautiful when made of entwined orange blossoms (which symbolize fertility and happiness). A double rosary lasso may also be given by one set of the parents and may be blessed with holy water three times in honor of the Trinity. A special person/couple places the lasso around the shoulders of the bride and groom, groom's shoulders first. The lasso may also be tied around their wrists. The couple wears the lasso throughout the remainder of the service. (The loop is symbolic of their love which should bind the couple together everyday as they equally share the responsibility of marriage for the rest of their lives.) At the end of the ceremony, the lasso is removed by either the couple which placed the lasso on the couple, or the priest. The lasso is given to the Bride as a memento of her becoming the mistress of the groom's heart and home."

The rich liturgical significance of this custom demonstrates a wonderful understanding of the symbolism of the rosary. Rather than simply seeing the rosary as a handy way to keep count of personal prayers, the custom of the Mexican wedding lasso brings essential aspects of the literal rosary — an unbroken circle of interconnected beads — and puts it to liturgical use as a symbol of how marriage is a union in every sense of the term: a union of two people, a union of two people with a community; a union of God with humanity. I recall in this regard the explanation I received in catechism of the Roman Catholic understanding of the Sacrament of Marriage, in which the priest explained to me how, in all the other six sacraments, the priest is the person who administers the sacrament as Christ to the recipient. He is the *persona Christi* — except for the Sacrament of Marriage, in which the individuals getting married instead are commissioned by the priest become the *persona Christi* for each other.

But the maternal symbolism of the Mexican wedding rosary is also impressive. The rosaries are given to the mothers, and as the rosary itself is essentially a devotion to the Blessed Mother, the custom discloses how much Mexican culture is conscious of mother as the source of life, and specifically of Mary as the Mother of God Incarnate. I also think that the use of the rosary in the context of the marriage ceremony is meant to enact in symbolic form how during a marriage the couple and their families will experience, as Mary did, the full fifteen mysteries of

Christ's life: the anticipation of birth, the sharing of love in the Visitation, the creation of a new generation of humanity entering into the world as simultaneously a cause for joy, an occasion for suffering, a chance for redemption and immortal life.

As I made plans to string the rosary of pearls and ivory, I was curious whether this rather profound liturgical symbolism ever gets explained to the couple. I could provide them with an opulent *lazo* they would surely cherish, but the real richness would be in understanding the way in which the rosary they wore would be a rosary they were living, both in the ritual and in their life together that followed.

The Lord is with you.

After the birth of our third child, Grace, in 1997, the rosary was such a comfort to us in a time of tremendous trial. Grace was born on December 23, and we brought her home from the hospital on Christmas day. What a tremendous gift for all of us she was! Her big sisters Hannah, age four, and Honor, age two, could hardly contain their excitement about this wonderful Christmas-time blessing.

Only three weeks or so later did we realize that little Gracie was not gaining weight, and because she was a nursing baby, there was no real way to quantify how much she was getting to eat. So, after some discussion with the doctor, it was decided that we would come in frequently for weight checks. After a couple of weight checks, she wasn't gaining and she was having bowel trouble. She cried a lot, and we all felt like we were failing her. We were sent to Riley Children's Hospital in Indianapolis—three hours away—not knowing whether we would just be there for the day, for a visit or for surgery—maybe two weeks maybe more.

At this point, the rosary had not been my devotion of choice for a very long time, and my husband had never really been comfortable with it. But at that time, we began to pray the rosary together. I see now how much we needed to pray together. We had started our relationship together by praying, but here we were, so stressed out, unable to even think of how to pray or what to pray for. So we began to pray the rosary together, and through God's blessing and Mary's protection, Gracie slowly began to get better.

The rosary was such a unexpected blessing to the two of us at that time. Even though neither of us had prayed the rosary much, it came to us and gave us a way to pray at a crucial time in our lives. It brought us such peace, and through this trial, we became stronger in our faith. Mother Mary continues to guide, protect, and heal our family.

Blessed are you among women...

"A baby and a tiny child receives God through his mother. His attitude to her is subjective, an innocent selfishness; he is aware of her simply as a part of himself, his bodily comfort, warmth, food, and sleep.... By the time he comes to the age of reason all these things and more gather together and merge into one idea, which includes everything – Home. To a young child, home stands for God. In it he learns to see and touch the gifts of God. If his mother is wise she will make his home beautiful. She will copy the world's creator and make a tiny new Eden. She will bring in flowers and give the child animals and feed the birds. The food on the table will be clean and simple and good. It will not only taste nice, it will look nice. From all this the child will learn naturally that God did not make the hideous travesty that we have made of created things.... 'Consider the lilies of the field' does not only mean enjoy their brief loveliness, but discover the lyrical quality of the love that has strewn them under your feet."

This passage from Caryll Houselander banished whatever doubts I had about my sudden awareness of Mary as a person in her own right. I knew, as I came to a deeper acquaintance with her through the rosary that she was slowly transforming my soul. So all my Protestant misgivings about being distracted from Jesus into an unhealthy Marian piety were easy to dismiss. I was coming to know a profound inner peace for the first time in many years. I had a sense of emotional containment and balance. When asked about my rosary practice and devotion to Mary, I would often say, "It's like I have finally found a source of true spiritual nourishment." Seeing Jesus through his mother's eyes, particularly the child Jesus, was one way in which the joyful mysteries of the rosary led me into a fuller intimacy with my savior that I had never had.

But why all this was happening, the reason behind Mary's singular transformative action in my interior life, finally became clear with the above passage, making me with my masculine blinkers feel just a little foolish. Of course, it is through a mother's love that we all first come to know God. Of course she is our first acquaintance with being fed, being satisfied, being held, knowing rest, seeing beauty. As we grow up and separate from our mothers, that small child in us does not disappear. The memory of those experiences of providence remain and resonate, persist through our mothers as the link to a cosmic experience of being cared for by the source of our being.

For this reason, too, I found my qualms about the phrase "Mother of God" dropping away. Admittedly, it is a rather blunt description, easily distorted, and despite all my studies, I remain somewhat astonished that so many learned theologians would become so entangled in literalisms and thereby miss the simple plain feminine wisdom it expresses: Mary bears God to us, as all our mothers do. Through our mothers we first experience the transcendent, the mystery of knowing our own source of being, the unbreakable bond of love that sustains our very life.

and blessed is the fruit of your womb, Jesus.

I don't have children of my own, so the mystery of the Nativity is my favorite, because I take the time when contemplating that mystery to bring to mind all the various "spiritual children" I have had over the years—kids I have taught, people who have come to me for mentoring, neighbors, godchildren. I try to bring them all to mind one by one and that's when I realize that I really don't have enough room in ten beads. And so I like to think this is how Mary reminds me of my own creativity and fertility. It's very gentle, very indirect, of course, but anyone who knows her recognizes how she works. She is like the most tactful, loving mother any of us have. She'd never say, "Oh don't worry about the fact you are over forty, not married. You're probably never going to have a family." No, instead, she makes room for me to quietly bring to mind all the children in spirit I have had, lets me remind myself of the abundance of blessing in my own life, while she just stands nearby, smiling.

Holy Mary...

I was adopted at a very early age from Brazil. My mother described me as a blessing in her life, because I was an answer to her prayers. She and my father had had trouble having a baby, so they decided to adopt a child, and my mother told me she prayed long and hard to have a child, until, lo and behold, the answer to her prayers was me. She also told me I was a blessing because I taught her about being a good parent. I taught her the capacity to love someone. When I heard my mother speak this way, I realized just how special I was to her, but not just to her—special to God, too, since I was the answer to their prayers.

When I was born to my birth mother, she wasn't able to keep me, because she was born into poverty herself and didn't have enough money to support me and give me adequate shelter, clothing, and education. So she decided that adoption would be the best way for me to receive all the things necessary for me to live a happy and good life. It must have given her a lot of sorrow and was probably the hardest thing she ever had to do. And yet, it must also have given her joy to know I was going to be in a better situation and have a good life.

So when I think of the mystery of the Nativity, I say, "Thank you, God, for letting my birth mother make the right choices in her life. Let her realize that what she did was the right thing, no matter what pain it caused her. Only you are capable of letting such a wonderful thing happen. This was truly a blessing for me."

Mother of God . . .

There is a fertility about Mary that no amount of emphasis on her virginity can possibly diminish, and until reading Beverly Donofrio's memoir *Looking for Mary,* I thought we rosary-makers were the only ones who had had the experience of Mary mystically multiplying in our lives. Indeed, it was a bit of an in-joke between us all that once you got started making rosaries, you might as well get used to the fact that pretty soon you'd be swimming in them. But here is Donofrio describing in her memoir of conversion how the purchase of a single, somewhat kitschy image of the Blessed Virgin Mary led to a semi-obsession with collecting images of Mary until she finally says, "I'd made a shrine of my house."

In the midst of my regular afternoon meditation, I realized that an outsider might well say the same about my house. I had images of the Blessed Mother — and sometimes more than one — in every single room of my house, except the bathroom, and, going one step beyond, I had many times more rosaries than that similarly scattered about, most of which I had made myself. Rosaries in bowls, rosaries on shelves, rosaries on tables. People don't believe us rosary-makers when we say that we have literally dozens of rosaries, but the researcher in me wanted to verify that this wasn't just my own idiosyncratic imagination, so I took a poll in our rosary-makers online group and sure enough, out of seventeen respondents, nearly half reported having twenty-five to one hundred rosaries in their home.

The phenomenon of the multiplying Marys illustrates what my spiritual director has repeatedly said to me and what the beautiful mystery of the Nativity likewise offers each of us in our contemplation. As I have sat in conversation, trying to discern whether or not a certain inspiration, image or experience is of divine origin, Chris reminds me to pay attention to the quality of the energy. "Divine energy is always creative," he says, a piece of wisdom I have come to know is true through my rosary-making.

My fertility, like Mary's, wasn't consciously intended. What started mostly as a kind of an experiment — being impressed with the beauty of the rosaries as made by certain craftspeople, I took it upon myself to see if I could rise to challenge of putting together my own rosaries with similar flair and devotion. And the result has been a burst of creative energy for me, fertile in every sense of the term — spiritually, as my prayer life has deepened; materially, as I am able to provide the rosaries I make to people to help them in turn deepen their own prayer lives; socially, as I am brought more fully into the body of Christ through my friendship with other rosary-makers and rosary-prayers. This fertility, inner and outer, personal and interpersonal, is the most convincing proof to me of the action of God's grace through me and this particular craft.

pray for us sinners now...

I know this might sound strange, but whenever I have money anxieties, I take my beads and pray the Joyful Mysteries. Our culture is so materialistic, and we're constantly told that "success" has to do with things, prestige, financial security. It's hard to resist buying into it, and then, when you are in business for yourself, with all the normal ups and downs, it's doubly hard to keep a spiritual perspective. But then, with the help of the Blessed Mother through the rosary, I am reminded that great things do happen to simple, faithful people.

I can see them so clearly when I contemplate the mystery of the Nativity. Here they are, the Holy Family, poor working-class folks, and something entirely new and different has come into the world through them, not because they were rich or powerful, but really because of the opposite. Because Mary and Joseph had so little and their faith was all they had, God chose to humble himself and come to us all as a tiny little baby born in a shed by the side of the road. When I get done with those mysteries about Jesus' early life and most of the time, I feel calm and clear, able to forget that business is down or that unexpected expenses have come up for us. If the Holy Family can do it on the power of faith, so can I and my family. And look what came out of their faith. The world has been changed.

and at the hour of our death.

For all the wisdom of cycling through the mysteries each week, I have enough of a rebellious streak, enough of a taste for innovation and creativity to imagine that perhaps some of the little-t traditions of Catholicism could be – or even, at times, should be – tweaked now and then. And so it was last Advent when I decided to devote my daily rosary to a contemplation of nothing other than the Joyful Mysteries, beginning with the official start of the Christmas season, after Vespers on the night before the first Sunday of Advent, and ending some six delicious weeks of festivity later, after singing the last note of compline on the last night of the octave of Epiphany in the courtyard of St. Albert's.

Surely the sorrowful mysteries could wait for a faraway Lent. For now we all were preparing for Christmas, as we bowed before a tabernacle swaddled in lilac velvet, watching the immense red bows on the pine swags flutter when the heat came on; as I kneaded the glossy dough of a dozen or so panettones I made for friends and loved ones in a burst of enthusiastic baking; as we stacked the cards we received on the mantle until it became a logistical challenge to accommodate all those images of Madonna and Child tucked in between Santas, sleighs, and snow scenes.

I didn't think either Jesus or Mary would mind too terribly much if I fasted from penitence and passion for now and let the inner light of hope and gratitude illuminate the darkness of winter afternoons. Meditating day after day upon their most joyful time together, each day of the season became filled with their presence, and the effect was cumulative, liberating, enlivening. Could this be wrong, to be so indulgent, to join myself so unstintingly with the Holy Family in the bliss of a new baby, a child of the Spirit? I assuaged my guilt by remembering that St. Francis, whose intense asceticism was mystically married to an equally ecstatic love of the created world, enjoined his brothers not just to put away their fasting and to feast but to smear meat upon the very walls in celebration of the extravagant, indulgent, wholly awe-inspiring generosity of God's gift of his Son.

There would be plenty of time to be sad and sorry in the coming year. For now, for this Christmas season, I prayed, let Christ be born each day, for me and for the world.

Amen.

Presentation

And when the time came for their purification according to the law of Moses, they brought him up to Jerusalem to present him to the Lord (as it is written in the law of the Lord, "Every male that opens the womb shall be called holy to the Lord"). …And his father and his mother marveled at what was said about him; and Simeon blessed them and said to Mary his mother, "Behold, this child is set for the fall and rising of many in Israel." (Luke 2:22-23; 33-34)

Hail, Mary . . .

A priest I know sent me a thank-you card with a very contemporary image of the Holy Family. On the back, it spoke of the Holy Family in terms that surprised me a little, because this particular priest is not really all that liberal, but due to his mission work among the poor, I think he has an attitude different from most middle-class folks. The card talked of the Holy Family in ways that I could relate to from my neighborhood: she's a pregnant, unmarried teenager, he's that kind of strange older guy who's willing to do the right thing when most men wouldn't have nothing to do with her, and then you have to think about what kind of life that baby of hers is going to have. There are a lot of families just like that in my experience. I mean, I really can look right out my window up and down the street, naming them.

So that's what I do when I'm praying the Presentation mystery: think about all those kinds of families and ask Mary to present them to God for help. Lord knows there really isn't a whole lot of help coming for them from down here on earth. Lots of words and lots of welfare regulations but not a whole lot of help. So I figure if she can gather all those families up into her arms and bring them into the Temple of God's presence, with Joseph standing next to her, maybe there's a chance for them, you know?

full of grace...

In my creativity, I am brought into even more intimate knowledge of God's creativity, and in this way, I dare to think that my rosary-making acquaints me in some small measure with Mary's experience of letting the Holy Spirit flow into and through her, transforming her life, her history, her hopes and dreams. Rosary-making can be a process of prayerful surrender to inspiration that gives way to something new and tangible, but then, to follow this image to its logical conclusion would be to say that the rosary itself is Jesus in a symbolic way, that we hold Jesus in our hands when praying the rosary in the way that Mary held him in her arms. I don't know if that is entirely too far off the mark, as long as we understand that we are speaking in symbols. When blessed, the rosary becomes a sacramental — an object consecrated to dispose us to the reception of grace — so to draw the parallel between ourselves and the Blessed Mother doesn't seem all that audacious, but rather almost the point. If the purpose of the Incarnation was to bring us all into more intimate acquaintance with the Creator of the world and all things in it, then Mary and the rosary, her devotion, indeed have a special part to play in this process of redemption. On Saturdays at morning prayer, we sing, "Come, let us worship God who holds the world and its wonders in his creating hand," a line that has special meaning to me as a rosary-maker, holding my own little pieces of wonder in my own creating hands, and offering my own dim experience of what it is like to be a creator back to God in prayer of praise and thanksgiving.

the Lord is with you.

I started rosary-making about five years ago when I couldn't find a rosary in a color that I liked. What I didn't know was that it's a lot more challenging than I expected. I had been an art major and have a fair bit of skill, but I didn't realize that everything worked best with special rosary-making tools. My first one, I have to admit, was pretty darn scary. I had loops of every size and shape, going here and there, and for the life of me, I couldn't figure out why it wasn't coming together. Only then did I figure out my everyday needle-nose pliers just wouldn't cut it. So I have officially dubbed my first rosary "Old Uggo," and I only haul it in extreme emergencies when people are saying a rosary and I haven't got one on me. Old Uggo will go down in history.

As I got more into it, I started looking around at the crosses and centers I could get a hold of. Most times, the casting was very beautiful, but they were generally made of base metal, and I didn't really think they looked all that attractive as they were. So I begin to paint the part, using regular latex paint at first, and sometimes glass staining in the background, finishing them with resin so they would last. In fact, one of the first ones I did was the San Damiano crucifix, which is very complex to paint. I must have done okay with it because I managed to get a papal blessing on it. I sent it to the pope, and the blessing came back from one of his secretaries, saying the Holy Father was very pleased.

At Christmastime in 2001, I was inspired to send one to Sophia Loren. I had just gotten this very, very strong urge one day to send this particular rosary to her. I hadn't really even been thinking about her, and to this day, I don't really myself know what the purpose of it was. It was after September 11, and I realized that there are so many people who do so many wonderful things that we never even think about thanking them for. Plus I always felt bad for her when she and her husband, Carlo Ponti, were excommunicated by Pope John XXIII because they married. I remember thinking to myself that, if they had just been ordinary people on the street, they might not have gotten absolution but they wouldn't have been excommunicated. Anyway, in the note I told her that I thought that was terrible and I sent her the rosary. That very same week, I got a really sweet note back from her, quite formal and short, but beautiful. She thanked me for the lovely rosary and she said that I hope my family and I would have a very Merry Christmas and a Happy New Year. When I told my priest what I had done, he was very pleased and said to me that he imagined by now the pope has forgiven them for all of that.

I have also done two rosaries for the actress Roma Downey, and she, too, wrote back to thank me. I'm not really the rosary-maker to the stars, though, because on that one, it was a very different situation. It wasn't just an urge. Since 1997, I have received locutions, that is to say, specific words and messages, from Our Lady, and with such locutions, you cannot deny it. It's beyond an urge. It has an urgency about it that makes you communicate what you have been told to the person meant to hear it, and it's very uncomfortable to do something like this for a celebrity. Even when I have received a locution for someone I know, I feel a little on edge, so when I have to do this for someone I don't know, it can be very uncomfortable.

Luckily for me, Roma Downey was very touched by the gift and the message, but for me, I didn't really have a choice. I was even told by Our Lady how to make the rosaries for her: they were both to be green, one in emerald green, with an aurora borealis finish and glass round beads, the other a little bigger with more nugget-shaped beads. Both were to have Celtic crosses painted emerald green and orange, and for the corpus I used natural colors, as I usually do. The center pieces were St. Patrick. The larger of the two was supposed to go to her brother who is a priest.

Since I'm not allowed to retain the message for the person once I have delivered it, I really don't know if the message pertained to her personal life or her professional activities. I couldn't tell you what it was now. I'm glad to have heard back from her that it was something that pleased her, whatever it was.

Blessed are you among women...

"The ordering of time, which seems so simple, really requires great skill and energy from the mother. It has tremendous importance, above all if it is related, as it obviously should be, to the rhythm of day and night and is interwoven with prayer. The child should wake with the singing of birds (and they sing in the cities as well as in the woods). Give his heart to God, when light is young, play for long hours when the world is awake and lively. He should form habits of regular hunger and thirst, so that food and hunger come together, and his grace is a real thanking. With twilight there should come stillness in the house and he should be lit to bed by the stars. From such ordering of time he will learn unconsciously, though it may be many years before he thinks this out, that he is not part of the chaos that man has made of this world, with its fearful abuse of time, but part of an ordered plan of love."

Indeed, it was many years before I "thought this out" for myself, as Caryll Houselander says in the above passage. In fact, it wasn't until after the rosary had already accomplished its subtle, inexorable ordering of time and attention in my life that I meditated upon the notion that the order of the cosmos, especially in its cycles of birth, death, and rebirth, flows from the feminine nature of God, rather than from God's masculinity. Acknowledging my own culture-bound ways of perceiving gender, nevertheless, I think of masculinity as linear, a movement from "here to there," directed, phallic. On the other hand, Mother Nature, around us and in us, seems instead to run in long, regular, almost eternal circles—the orbits of the planets, the cycles of the day and night, hunger and satiation, monthly cycles of fertility and quiescence, daily cycles of excitation and rest.

And in this cyclical ordering of our time, in making ritual of the human experience, it is God the Mother who is revealed. That is why I think the unbroken circle of the rosary is so profoundly comforting. Through such a cyclical form of prayer — fingers following the path till the end meets the beginning, only to begin again, each cycle of each mystery part of a larger cycle of a set of mysteries, each set of Aves defining a period of contemplation, a swatch of time, regular and recurrent within the rosary, taken up each day — through this ordering of time we come to know more intimately what Mary's singular grace revealed to us: that God comes to us through womanhood, through the unique acquaintance with the cycles of birth and death that women know.

Thus even the very shape of the rosary evokes for me a sense of touching the infinite womanliness of God—to hold the endless circle and allow my prayer life to order my time, day by day, hour by hour, minute by minute. As the divine office orders the time and thereby the life and soul of the monastic, so this lay psalter of the rosary orders the time, and thereby the lives and souls of lay people, in the irresistible and ineffably comforting way in which the mother orders the time and thereby the life and soul of her child—waking, playing, eating, sleeping. This supremely feminine action of the Divine is indeed the special way in which Mary, mother of Christ, enables us to get at a very mysterious truth often hidden by the sexism of the tradition, reveals in her maternal nurture a way for us, indeed, to make a mother of God.

and blessed is the fruit of your womb, Jesus.

"The images that he used evoke picture after picture of his home life. As you listen to him, you can almost see the grave little boy watching his mother with the absorbed interest that children always bring to skilled work beautifully done, watching her cook and sweep and bake, put the oil in the lamps, light the candles and bottle the wine.

"Listen to some of his images: you cannot mend an old garment with a new piece of cloth. (How many men would know that?) You cannot put new wine into old bottles. Then cleansing of cups and platters, which is just washing up. The candle set high to light the whole room, the sweeping of the house, the annoyance of rust and the inevitable moth! Children clamoring for food and the parents who know how to give good gifts to their children. The oil for the lamps and the leaven put into the bread for the baking."

Is this housewifeliness of Mary, described so affirmatively here, the same quality which leads my Dominican friends to be so fond of calling Mary the "first contemplative" of the Christian tradition? I think so. Through the rosary, I have become familiar with the essential characteristics of contemplative living: an appreciation of the small and simple, a willingness to attend to what is necessary each day, an ability to sense the divine in humble, everyday pleasures.

The beads are so small in my big man's hands and nothing particularly flashy, and yet each of them represents a brief, humble, direct way of addressing God in prayer. If it is possible to take each bead and make it be an occasion of awareness of the divine — and it has been for me, by the grace of God — then it is likewise possible to take each small daily task and make it a similar occasion. Indeed, the beads have worked over the years to wean me very slowly away from that craving for stimulation and novelty that is so innate to my personality and so heavily reinforced by our consumer culture. They have brought me to what Jesus undoubtedly did see in Mary's work about the home: that God is not just in the mountaintop or the temple, but likewise in the details of ordinary life.

Humility is the gate to all virtues, after all, and using the rosary to meditate with gratitude upon the simple pleasures of everyday life, I have found a way to practice humility, to keep my attention and my sense of self close to the ground. The rosary has been so helpful to me in this practice of humility, and for the very reason that Houselander gives voice to: for all his cosmic glory and for all the majesty the Church loves to put forward on Jesus' behalf, the rosary shows us the other side of his nature, his everyday humanity: his childhood, his vulnerability, his peasant simplicity — the humblest aspects of his life on earth, seen most sharply and appreciated most lovingly through the eyes of none other than his mother.

My aspirations toward sanctity find their most grandiose expression through a contemplation of Christ's divinity, but how often I have found all of that ambitiousness a spiritual dead-end, reinforcing my pride and spiritual materialism and thus leading me away from him in the end, blocking my way by puffing up my own sense of self. Instead, I can take up the rosary daily, spend time in repetitive, simple prayer, detach from the glory, come home to Mary, and let her housewifeliness lead me back to Jesus the man, her son whom she loved and bathed and fed and rocked and taught. I can let her suggest that Jesus might be found in my own routine, in an appreciation of my own little home, in the small ordinary graces that come through my daily work, through kindness to strangers, through boring tasks made into occasions of prayer. This school of humility through the rosary has been enormously fruitful in my spiritual life, for "Christ did not deem equality something to be grasped at, but rather he emptied himself out and took the form of a servant" (Phil. 2:6–11). The rosary helps me, too, to empty myself and to live contemplatively, seeing and responding promptly and fully to whatever the necessity is that presents itself in my day-to-day life. In this way, I have made the decade of the Presentation a meditation upon the life of the child Jesus, bringing myself to know God as a child, through the humble, prayerful domesticity of his mother's home and his father's work.

Holy Mary . . .

The Presentation mystery draws me frequently to meditate upon the graces I received through my baptism. Since I was made a member of the Church as a baby and spent my life within the faith, I sometimes forget what a great blessing it is to be a member of a community sharing one baptism, one faith, and one life. When praying, I try to call to mind the many ways in which this communion has been my salvation throughout my life, how the sacraments have sustained me within and without during tough times, how I have brought all my joys and sorrows to God through the faith communities I have known. I, too, in my own little way, represent a portion of the mystical body of Christ, because I have been baptized. I use the Presentation mystery to strengthen my discernment of how his mystical body is at work in the world still, through me personally and through the larger community of the Church.

Mother of God

Another aspect of rosary-making that I am particularly fond of is the way each rosary engages me in a dialogue between tradition and innovation. Certain parts of the design are given and must be respected, and yet once in place, the challenge, for me as a designer, is how I can do something new and different, make a type of rosary that has never yet been seen before and which still remains faithful to the spirit of contemplation, prayer, and devotion to the Blessed Mother. Some of the craftspeople I know have gotten *very* creative, using all sorts of natural materials for beads — flower buds, shells, seeds — thinking way outside of the box and pushing the look of the traditional rosary to its limit. My own feeling is that a rosary is meant to be used for prayer and praise, so while I think it might be quite innovative to make a rosary from feathers or little balls of laundry lint, I bump up against the salutary limitation provided by the spiritual tradition in which the rosary-making resides as a devotion and as a craft. Rosaries, however artistic they might be, aren't just art objects, nor should they be. And I have seen some outlandish rosaries. For a while, on eBay a metal artist was auctioning off a huge sculpture of a rosary that he had fashioned by welding cannonballs and boat-chain together, an unwieldy creation that I had a very hard time imagining gracing any kind of sacred space. It is somewhat unfashionable to allow tradition to dictate very much to us as contemporary Americans, since the United States so prides itself on its culture of continual self-reinvention, but in a craft tradition within a religion, perhaps, tradition serves to connect, to support and, yes, to challenge. So rosary-making for me is a microcosm of what it means to be a Roman Catholic, to reside in a long and well-established tradition with specific forms and rituals to be honored, and yet, to bring my own particular gifts and individuality to bear on that tradition, to help that tradition develop and change. That's why I like it when someone at church sees one of my rosaries and looks quizzically, half-smiling, a little surprised. "I don't think I've ever seen a rosary like that," they sometimes say. "It's really striking." And yet, they know it's a rosary. I see their fingers naturally go to the cross, to the center, play over the beads. All of that says to me that I've been able to advance the tradition a little, to help people see this beautiful old devotion in a new and different way, to show people that the rosary, like our whole spiritual tradition, like all of God's whole creation, is in a state of evolution, continually inspired, continually revealing, changing and growing, organic and miraculous.

pray for us sinners now...

In English we call her Our Lady of Good Counsel, but in Latin her title in the litany is actually Mother of Good Counsel, *mater boni consilii,* which is a slight difference but one that means a lot to me. Our parish has a little shrine to her where I go to pray, and I've said many rosaries in front of her image and have received much good advice. Being a social worker, for better or worse, I'm in the advice business, and yet, frequently the situations that I encounter are not ones that are easily solved, if at all. For a time I worked for an HIV agency and before that a hospice, and it can get very depressing and overwhelming, even though I do have a lively faith and good support. But sometimes, people come with needs for which there are just no resources, or, as in my previous work, they come with a terminal illness and there is nothing to be done.

That's when I go and pray to my Mother of Good Counsel, and usually I pray on the Joyful Mysteries because those are the ones that give me the most hope in the darkness. In the image of her at our parish shrine, she holds the baby Jesus very tenderly, so as I pray before her, I concentrate on how it would feel to let her hold me, hold all of us like that, with love and tenderness.

and at the hour of our death.

I confess to being very literal sometimes about the rosary mysteries. Perhaps I have been overly influenced by some of the pictorial representations to which I have been exposed over the years, so for me the Presentation mystery is primarily about handing on the faith tradition that has shaped my life. The rosary is an ingenious, or perhaps I should say, inspired way to trace out the narrative arc of Jesus' life through the eyes of Mary, so I tend to adhere quite faithfully to praying the sets of mysteries in order. In the Presentation, I really feel the spiritual weight of all this history. We have the little baby Jesus being brought to the Temple by his youngish mother with the witness of his slightly older father and receiving the blessing of the elders, with a touch of prophecy for the future thrown in for good measure. It's as if all the generations past and future come together in this picture of the Presentation, so I generally pray for my elders in faith as well as those yet unborn to whom, God willing, I will hand on the tradition. My faith connects me to the past and to the future. Taking some time on a regular basis to let that historical sense of things sink in is a good thing for all of us, for our own souls and for the world around us. It keeps us respectful, grounded, and other-directed. It makes us more like Christ.

Amen.

Fifth Joyful Mystery

Finding in the Temple

*After three days they found him in the temple, sitting among
the teachers, listening to them and asking them questions;
and all who heard him were amazed at his understanding
and his answers. And when they saw him, they were astonished; and his mother said to him, "Son, why have you treated
us so? Behold your father and I have been looking for you
anxiously." And he said to them, "How is it that you sought
me? Did you not know that I must be in my Father's house?"
And they did not understand the saying which he spoke to
them ... and his mother kept all these things in her heart.*

(Luke 2:46-51)

Hail, Mary...

Another journey, this one to Jerusalem. Jesus decided at age
twelve or so to deliver a sermon in the Temple. His words were
well received, but he hadn't told Mary and Joseph of his where-
abouts, and they were really concerned that he was lost. When
they were reunited, his words, "Did you not know that I must
be about my Father's business," could almost be paraphrased,
"You know, Mom and Dad, I'm not a kid anymore!"

When I pray on this mystery, I think of the time my own children were adolescents. I needed to remind myself then — and
even now sometimes even despite the fact they are grown up —

that I am only a parent, a caregiver for a brief period. Our children are here to pursue the business God has given them to do in the world.

full of grace . . .

Rosary-making, perhaps like any craft, is an experience of birth, a process of conceiving, gestating, putting forth, and letting go. When I get together with other rosary-makers, we joke about how our favorite rosary is always the last one we made. Those of us who have children find it very easy to identify the same proprietary feelings. You feel responsible for the creation of this unique and individual beauty, and yet at the same time, you are awed, because you are not really, fundamentally, responsible. You see how a certain kind of grace or miracle or fertility has come through you and produced this lovely individual who now in her turn graces the earth with her life. That's why rosary-makers always have oodles and oodles of rosaries. Like children, they are difficult to let go of.

the Lord is with you.

It's so convenient to have ten fingers. I can't always fish the rosary out of my pocket. I have to hold on to the seat handle as I stand on the subway, or my arms are full of packages as I wait in line. But my fingers are there pressing out the Hail Marys, one by one, and I wonder if this is the optimal way to say the rosary. Probably not. Will I find the time today to do the full-on, sit-a-decade, kneel-a-decade, stand-a-decade routine of my parochial school years? Probably not. So instead, I do what I can — keep my mind on the subject of each mystery, announce it to myself as I begin the "Our Father." Not being good at visualization, I conjure up images of the famous paintings: Jesus kneeling in the garden of Gethsemane, leaning on a huge boulder and looking heavenward; Mary being spirited up by angels, leaving roses in her coffin. Each mystery has its picture, but after about the third "Hail Mary," my mind wanders off, and I have to pull it back.

For all my struggles and imperfections, though, one thing is true: the rosary reminds me of my connection to God through the examples set by Jesus and Mary, and the formal prayer of the rosary satisfies my need to connect with God, anywhere, anytime, and especially when I'm not able to compose a more personal original prayer.

Blessed are you among women...

Last year was so filled with such terrible scandal in the Church. Nothing I myself haven't really known about, I am sorry to say — growing up and going through Catholic school, most of us knew which fathers to trust and which ones to keep your distance from. Nevertheless, it is disheartening to see the whole sordid mess plastered on the front page of the newspaper day after day, and to feel in some way, as a Catholic, connected and identified with such a collective failure. Ultimately, I think the publicity is for the good, since the truth will set us free. I look at how twenty-five years of inaction have finally resulted in a few swift months of much better action and discussion, due to a healthy dose of exposure to public opinion.

Anyway, back to the rosary. I found myself spontaneously meditating about finding Jesus in the Temple in connection with this sexual-abuse scandal. When I'm contemplating this mystery, I pray to the Virgin as the Seat of Wisdom and think about how she found Jesus teaching. So I do as she did, putting myself at his feet in my imagination, asking him questions, naming specific situations or issues and then listening to his answers. I try to make a seat for his wisdom and discernment in my own soul as she did in hers.

But last week, saturated in current Church events, it occurred to me while praying the rosary that another part of the mystery has to do with the adolescent Jesus getting lost in the Temple. It hit me that this aspect of the mystery perfectly sums up the present situation of the Church: Jesus the teenager has gotten lost in the huge, labyrinthine temple of the institutional Church's concern. By not being more active, Church officials, and we laypeople, too, have lost sight of the holiness of our children and our teenagers. In all the long, winding corridors of administrative power, doctrinal sophistry, and egotistical dedication to saving face, we have lost our dear, sweet, wise Jesus. Where is he? How do we find him? How did we lose him? Where were we looking when he slipped away and out of sight?

For me, the sexual-abuse issue was a watershed in my spiritual life. Never again will I be able to pray the fifth Joyful Mystery of the rosary without thinking about how easy it is to lose sight of Jesus in the Temple. I now pray that the Blessed Mother who found him will bring him back to us in the Church. As one of the more forthright of our local Dominican priests preached on the feast of the Visitation this year, is there any doubt that if women had been granted at least equal power and influence in the administration of the Church, that this whole current mess would never have happened? Imagine the Blessed Mother knowing about serial pedophilia and delaying a full and swift response out of concern for public relations or failing to immediately remove the offender, instead getting caught up in the niceties of canon law? It is unthinkable, really. It is this fierce, feminine, maternal attitude I see in this mystery now: Mary's Son has gotten lost, and on Mary we need to rely to find him and his wisdom again. I use this mystery now to pray for the institutional Church, for the Temple in which Jesus can both get lost and in which, when guided by the Seat of Feminine Wisdom, Jesus can also be found again.

and blessed is the fruit of your womb, Jesus.

When I meditate upon Jesus preaching in the Temple, I am reminded God gave me a good mind which I have tried to use to the best of my abilities. Using my mind, however, has led me to doubt aspects of religion. I know that I shouldn't have doubts, but I am very curious and I want to expand my mind. Sometimes, this caused my mother a little bit of pain, because she is a devout Christian, and there has never been a doubt in her mind about the existence of God.

Now I consider the gift of a good, sharp mind a grace from God, but I wonder whether or not the way I'm using it is always how God intended. Sometimes I feel it is just my personality that makes me want to question religion and the existence of God, but on the other hand, my questions are probably the same as a lot of teenagers: If there is a God, why is there pain and suffering? What is the meaning of life? Why were we created, and what is our purpose? I have been looking for God in many different places, and like Jesus, who was a teenager, too, the Church and my parents are major places where I have found God.

Holy Mary . . .

I was living with one of my brothers in an adult community located out in the southwestern part of New Jersey. He'd been widowed for about a year, and we hadn't lived under the same roof for over forty years. I had sold my own home because the cost of it was beyond my income, and the understanding with my brother was that I would buy our food while I stayed

73

with him and that my intention was to buy a home in the same adult community. However, since the age limit to live there was fifty-five, I would need to wait to close until my birthday in February. With all this understood, I moved in with him in July and everything seemed to be going well.

As Christmas approached, my brother became moodier by the minute. Asking him what was wrong didn't get me anything but grunts of "I don't feel well," which made some sense to me since he had some long-term physical ailments. I wasn't having much luck finding properties I could afford, though I really wanted to close on a house as soon as possible. The Saturday before Christmas, the tension I had been feeling from my brother came to head, when he started an argument with me and finished it with "You have to leave, now!" I tried to stay calm, since he had had one of these outbursts earlier and had said at the time that it had just been his way of dealing with his anger at his poor health. This time, I reminded him I couldn't close on a house before my birthday on February 17, but he said that was too long for him to wait and that I had to move out right way.

I went outside, sat in my car, and cried, not understanding why my brother was being so cruel so close to the holidays. With my limited income, I didn't have the money for a hotel or a furnished room. I'm a very independent person and can usually handle anything that comes my way, but here I was in a very tight situation and there didn't seem to be any way out that I could see.

Mary has always been the one I turn to when I can't seem to find my way no matter what the situation, so I sat there in my car and prayed to Mary for guidance. The rosary came to mind, but my entire home was in a storage unit, along with all my rosaries. The next day, I went over to the church store, and after looking at the rosaries on display—all of which were more than I could afford—I explained my circumstances and asked the man at the counter if there were others that weren't so dear. He led me to the rear of the store and showed me some rosaries. When I asked how much, he hesitated and then said, "One dollar." I couldn't believe my ears. "Really?" I asked. Yes, yes, he insisted, they're only one dollar.

I chose a white rosary, and, as I came to the register to pay, I asked if he knew if Father was in, so I could have my rosary blessed. He gestured and said, "Well, the monsignor is standing right behind you." I turned to see an elderly gentleman without a turned collar standing there. "Monsignor, could you bless this rosary for this lady?" The monsignor placed his hand over mine, and I felt a rush of energy from his hand as he blessed the beads. That night I lay on the bed in my room and prayed the rosary, feeling so close to Mary and knowing in my heart that somehow the situation would change and that I'd be able to have my own life again. And that's what happened: I found a house I could afford, put a down payment on it and closed on my home on February 19, two days after my fifty-fifth birthday.

Shortly after moving in, I was washing the kitchen cabinets without my glasses on, since I usually only use them for reading, when I pulled a cabinet door open and something swung in my face. Startled, I reached for my glasses and couldn't believe my eyes. It was a beautiful green crystal rosary! It had been left hanging on the door of the cabinet, and with the dark wood behind it, I hadn't noticed it. I called my realtor and asked her if she remembered seeing it when we were in the house for the closing. She said yes, but she didn't think to say anything; she thought it was a gift that had been left there by the previous owner.

I feel blessed: my neighbors are warm and welcoming people, the neighborhood is quiet and peaceful, and I have a home, not just a house. So yes, I believe in miracles. I believe in the power of prayer. I believe when we speak to the Divine, it hears us, but we don't immediately get what we want or "hear" the response. But if we wait and don't lose faith, eventually our prayers are answered and our needs will be met.

Mother of God . . .

I don't know why my friend Cristi sent this particular rosary to me, but it was the first rosary I ever had. She says Our Lady instructed her to do this for me, and, I can believe that because everything about the rosary was beautiful. I loved its dark green color, the rose beads she used with all the white in them, the gold, the beautiful crucifix. I loved the way it was sparkling at me when I first looked at it, and I especially loved the way it felt. It actually still makes my hands feel good when I hold it. It feels "right." Even now I still can't stop looking at it. Sometimes I hold it just to hold it. What is interesting about it, though, is I've noticed sometimes the rosary is dark, sometimes it's bright and shiny. I don't know why, but it changes, not based on my moods. I haven't made a correlation to anything yet, so that's still a mystery.

And the effect of this rosary? I used to build doll houses but after I began to pray with this rosary, I found I just wanted to make rosaries, mostly so I could somehow share the feeling Our Lady gave me with everyone. I really don't know how to describe this feeling, except to say that it is a feeling that takes you to another level. And you can't keep it to yourself. In fact, it gets stronger the more you share it.

For example, I took my rosary to my son's soccer games and showed it to friends everywhere I went. You can't believe how many men have pulled rosaries out of their pockets when I showed them mine, or how many have asked for a rosary. My eldest son was ten at the time. He just *had* to have one. Now, where does that feeling come from?

pray for us sinners now . . .

For the month of October, we have been asked to pray the decade of the rosary each night and to reflect on that particular mystery. When I get settled into bed every night, I usually begin to think about all the things I have to do and all the things I am worried about. So usually I can't get to sleep. But lately, it has been different. I remember that we are supposed to say the rosary, so I take some deep breaths and begin to recite the prayer. Sooner rather than later, I have fallen asleep. That's how it is with the rosary: I get a great sense of peace, and all my problems seem to be lifted away. Not only can the rosary be said for the whole world and for others, but also to help yourself.

and at the hour of our death.

We call them mysteries but it's easy to forget that the focus of the rosary meditations are in every sense real mysteries. I come back to that particular truth many times, not just in my own prayer on these episodes, but in a more mundane way. Roman Catholics have a special penchant for using particular words in ways different than their general definitions. "Ordinary" is one of those, especially in the phrase "ordinary time," which one would think means a period when nothing special is going on but which actually denotes the Church practice of numbering, or ordering, the Sundays. Another one is "decade" (and pronounced not "deck-aid" but "deckèd"), referring not to ten years but rather the group of ten beads on a rosary.

So, when people, usually non-Catholics, who have asked me about the rosary get a kind of glazed-over look in their eyes when I begin to speak of the mysteries that are the focus of meditation, I have to remind myself to back up. What we call "mysteries" most people would call "episodes in the life of

Christ," and in historical research on the development of the rosary, these are often referred to as the "*vita Christi* meditations" that were added in the Middle Ages to the pre-existing practice of reciting 150 Hail Marys on knotted prayer cords.

For all the translating that might be necessary, however, when I am trying to teach people the rosary, the fact that these episodes are called mysteries is a reminder of an important fact. When we turn our thoughts to the Annunciation, or Christ carrying the Cross, or the Assumption of Mary, we are not just sitting around thinking about the literal circumstances of historical occurrence: we are contemplating mysteries, which means we are presuming that historical occurrence is not all there is. Events from the life of Mary and Jesus also hold some sacred truth about the nature of God hidden within them, some wisdom or insight not yet fully disclosed to us, some lesson or experience of the Divine that remains "mysterious" still to our minds and hearts.

With our beads as our tool, we bring our awareness in the rosary, then, not just to events or episodes but to the mysteries of God's life on earth, praying not as rote habit but as a full-blown contemplative practice in search of continual revelation. The challenge that the word "mysteries" presents to those unfamiliar with the rosary, therefore, is a good one, as it requires a certain clarity of intention, makes one think a little, is even a bit humbling for those of us devotees. No matter how many years we pray the rosary, those mysteries will still always be that — mysterious. For who can know the mind of God?

Amen.

The Sorrowful Mysteries

Gethsemane

And then they went to a place which was called Gethsemane, and he said to his disciples, "Sit here, while I pray." And he took with him Peter and James and John, and began to be greatly distressed and troubled.... And going a little farther, he fell on the ground and prayed, "Abba, Father, all things are possible to thee. Remove this cup from me; yet not what I will, but what thou wilt." And he came and found them sleeping.... (Mark 14:32–33, 35–37)

Hail, Mary...

This gray, foggy February day is a mixed blessing. Because it is so cool, the walk up the hill to the rose garden is much easier and with a bit of exertion, I don't even really need my coat. On the other hand, I know from all the condensation forming on my sweater and the misty air leaving a damp sheen everywhere, that I better take care once I get there not to get a chill. So I pull my knit cap down over my ears and continue, looking forward to the deserted place.

Even in this wet winter, the tennis courts beside the terraces are sometimes ping-ponging with die-hard sports nuts, but not today. Today the courts are empty and, as I squeak open the gate, I can tell that I am alone here. The sloping hillside amphitheater, with its Arts-and-Crafts arbors and gravel walkways, host nothing but the roses — and now me, breathing a little heavily — and I find a spot to sit among the naked branches of all the carefully pruned bushes. The famous view of the Bay and the Golden Gate Bridge is obscured by fog so thick I wouldn't even know there was anything out there, nor are there any roses here, except in my memories of last summer and fall. Indeed, the only spot of color here is the deep purple of my amethyst rosary I take off from around my neck, my hands grateful for the warmth of the beads. As I gather my thoughts, preparing to contemplate the events of Christ's passion and death in this special place I come to for a midday miniretreat, I hear a little rustle of leaves down by the swollen creek. Without moving anything but my gaze, I see the two large dark eyes of a deer look up at me, both of us still, both of us slightly wary of the other, and she watches me as I smoothly lift the cross to my forehead and lips, beginning not with "In the name of . . . " but instead the familiar words of the Psalm, sung under my breath to the tune we use in morning prayer. "As a deer that yearns for running streams, so my soul is yearning for you my God."

full of grace . . .

For twenty years I ministered as a Roman Catholic priest, and during those years, I was privileged to enter people's lives and walk with them at very significant times and in ways most people never get an opportunity to do. One of those times is when a loved one died, when I would be asked to lead the prayers and preside at the funeral services.

Typically, Roman Catholics hold three services at the time of death — a Vigil Service, or as we used to call it years ago, a wake, usually held the night before; the funeral Mass or Mass of Christian Burial; and then, finally, the burial itself. At the wake, it was traditional for those gathered to pray the five decades of

82

the rosary, meditating on the sorrowful mysteries of the Lord's passion and death. Sometimes a few extra prayers were said, but for the most part, it was just the rosary. After the Second Vatican Council, however, many of these traditional practices of the Church began to change. The wake was transformed into what is now called a Vigil Service, with Scripture readings and a homily replacing the rosary, concluding with a few additional prayers. For many families, this new format seemed very foreign at the time and quite often a discussion would ensue prior to the Vigil Service between the family and the priest as to what would take place at the service: rosary or Liturgy of the Word? Because I was ordained well after Vatican II, by the time I was active in ministry, the Vigil Service with its Liturgy of the Word had become the accepted practice, and in some parishes had replaced the rosary altogether.

For me, personally, the rosary was never my prayer of choice; I had not been raised in a family that prayed the rosary every night, as was the practice in some Catholic families, and indeed, the only times I prayed the rosary were when I attended wakes with my parents. Was it those early experiences of the rosary at wakes that affected my decision years later as a priest to include the rosary as part of the Vigil Services that I led? Perhaps. I knew in my heart that most families desired the rosary devotion as part of the obsequies for their beloved deceased, and so once I was a priest, unless the family specifically asked for it to be excluded, I presided at a service that was a combination of rosary and Scripture service.

Though the rosary had not ever been my own favorite devotion, still, every time I led the congregation in the rosary, I did so slowly and deliberately, unlike most priests I had known. I would make a point to kneel at the coffin — not an easy thing to do for me because of my size and weight, not to mention the

wear and tear on my knees. While most of the congregation usually answered their halves of those prayers quickly and by rote,
I took my time. I would pronounce each word precisely so we
could all meditate upon what the prayers were saying, so we
could really contemplate the mysteries of the rosary that were
the focus of the prayers. Even if the Hail Mary was repeated
ten times each decade, I felt strongly that each prayer upon
each bead was a single prayer to God and to the deceased who
I now believed was with God, as well as for his or her eternal
rest. This added time and effort I took to pray the rosary slowly
and deliberately – the pain I had to endure, the discomfort
of attempting to fit on the prie-dieu obviously constructed for
someone much more petite than I – all became part of the Vigil
Service for me. They became prayers and sacrifices I counted
as additional offerings for the repose of the departed soul and
for the consolation of the family, mourning the loss of someone
they loved.

Many times I did not know the deceased or the family very
well, especially when I first arrived at a parish, but truly that
made no difference. I never looked upon my role merely as
presider – if I had, I would have stood through the entire service. Instead, I looked upon myself as one of the congregation,
and more importantly a member of the larger parish community, representing them to this family as it prayed for their loved
one who had gone before us. Most especially, however, I par-
ticipated in that prayer as a member of that family who knelt
behind me. Since they had given me the privilege of entering
their lives in such a special way, I felt part of them. Even if I had
never met them, I was not a stranger; they had invited me to preside at this service, and for that hour or so, I was more than
presider or priest – I was one of the family.

I have been to several Vigil Services since I left active ministry,
and the experience is entirely different. I am there as a part of

the family or friend of the decedent, and I usually know the person or at least a member of the family very well; sometimes the rosary is included and sometimes not. Each time I attend, however, I remember those rich experiences over that twenty-year period, when those families had invited me to be a part of them, and I was privileged to kneel, finger those beads, and pray the words of the Hail Mary.... prayers—slowly and deliberately.

the Lord is with you.

Praying is a universal language which helps all people communicate through God, a language that makes all of us God's people. So I do my part as a child of God and pray as much as possible. In religion class, we were given the assignment to pray the rosary, and after praying for six days, I feel a great burden has been lifted off my shoulders. I had a sense of belonging I hadn't known before and a kind of faith that all of my questions would eventually be answered, maybe not today or tomorrow, but someday. I also began to feel a kind of peace come over me. I feel better than I have in a very long time, both spiritually and physically.

What started as an assignment in class has ended for me in a spiritual awakening. As I have come to see through praying the rosary, only God can lead me to the answers I am seeking. Through the prayer the question is asked, and through prayer we are led to see God's way for us, which is the answer within.

Blessed are you among women...

Rosary-making requires patience. I usually begin a rosary with a vision. In my mind's eye, I can see a certain piece, made of these beads, this sort of center and cross, about this big. It is very clear to me usually, and I've even woken up having had a dream

85

of a new rosary design. But like most visions, material reality isn't always as cooperative as the imagination, and bringing that particular vision into practice can be very difficult. So I have to cultivate patience. Some rosaries have literally taken months and months to come together, sometimes just because the right part is out of stock and I need to wait, sometimes because the bead stores don't have precisely the sort of material I want.

I remember wanting to make a rainbow rosary for adults and having to look hard to find beads of six different colors that didn't end up looking like those on a circus clown or from a Crayola crayon box. After a week or two of ferreting around bead stores, I was able to assemble five of the six colors — carnelian red, yellow jade, green onyx, blue onyx, and amethyst purple, all natural stones. The colors looked good, not garish. But there I was and for the life of me I couldn't find the right orange, and without the orange there was no way to make a proper rainbow rosary. So once again, it was a matter of patience, waiting, waiting, until finally I managed to come upon a jasper that had just the right brick-orange.

Some rosaries are still waiting to come together in my boxes. Last year at a bead show I bought a couple of luscious strands of disk-shaped petrified wood, rich striated brown, smooth and heavy, but since then I have not been able to find the right centers and crosses to suit them, so I wait. As someone who generally shows very little patience about things (ask my friends and family!), I credit rosary-making nearly entirely with whatever modicum of patience I have managed to scrape together for myself at this point in my life.

and blessed is the fruit of your womb, Jesus.

I have a made a commitment to say the rosary each day and most days that isn't a problem, but you know, there are always "those days" when either life gangs up on me and there are a hundred thousand things to take care of. Or sometimes it is really me. I have the time earlier on but I keep thinking, "Oh it'll be nicer to say the rosary later, when I'm less preoccupied or rushed." It is supposed to be prayer after all, not punching a clock, so I only feel half-guilty when I'm not in the mood. Anyway, the day is over and I haven't said the rosary yet. I go off to bed with all of my best intentions and start off. And you know, what happens of course: I rarely get through two decades before I drift off to sleep. It is a lovely way to go to sleep, I must admit—sort of like being tucked in by the Blessed Mother the way my grandmother used to do with us kids. And being my compulsive self, I would make sure to continue saying the rosary, even part of a decade, if I woke up in the middle of the night, my little black rosary still in my hands.

I used to worry myself about this, as if I hadn't acted in my own best interest, waiting till the last minute of my day to say the rosary, knowing full well I would be too tired to stay awake. What good is falling asleep in the middle of the rosary doing for my faith life?

But maybe about a year ago, having woken up with my little black rosary still in my hands, I went to Mass on a Sunday morning, and that day we happened to sing Psalm 63: On my bed I remember you, on you I muse through the night. I thought to myself, "Maybe that's what I am doing, maybe I am 'musing through the night.'" Wouldn't "remembering God in my bed" look like what I was doing—falling asleep in prayer, waking up in mid-prayer, framing the night, in certain way, with prayer? "My soul clings to you, your right hand holds me fast." Perhaps I was returning the favor, my right hand holding the rosary fast through the night, clinging to God through prayer. That was a different way to look at it, rather than "couldst thou not watch with me one hour?" which is more my typical response. Instead,

I was "musing through the night," praying always, as St. Paul tells us to do.

I don't worry anymore about falling asleep during the rosary. In fact, sometimes I even look forward to gently resting in the arms of Mary, holding her beads the whole night long, waking up a little bit, remembering the mysteries, saying a prayer or two before falling back to sleep.

Holy Mary . . .

I had never heard of anyone else praying the rosary on their hands until I read *Silence* by Shusaku Endo, a gripping contemporary novel based on a real trio of eighteenth-century Jesuit missionaries martyred in Japan. In it, two Portuguese missionaries go to Japan, ostensibly to revive the Christian community there abandoned by its founder who apostatized under torture. After landing in secret and spending some weeks trying to elude the authorities by hiding under the floor of a peasant hut, one of them prays the rosary using his fingers to count out the prayers.

I have been doing that for years, and I didn't know until reading that novel that anyone else had ever even thought of it. I don't count by sticking my fingers out, in one-potato, two-potato fashion. Instead, in a spontaneous way, I came upon the custom of making a little circle of my thumb and my fingers, which in my imagination is like the circle of the rosary. I couldn't really tell you when I started, but now I typically do it in public situations, like in traffic, or waiting in line or other places when I don't have my rosary beads on my person. I like the idea of not just praying the rosary but actually turning my body into the rosary itself with this gesture. I don't know, maybe that is a little too abstruse, but I like that symbolism. One place I very often say the rosary in this way is—you may not believe this—but at the gym, when I'm doing the LifeCycle or the Stairmaster. I get up very early, so I am often completely alone in the aerobic room at 5:30 a.m., and it's the perfect time to meditate. I close my eyes, loop my fingers this way over the hand grips, starting with my right hand and going to the left the way I would pray the rosary with a set of beads, and let myself and my prayers fall into the rhythm of the cycling and the hum of the ventilation system. I can't really imagine swinging a set of rosary beads around a gym, and I've sometimes thought it is kind of a neat coincidence that God gave us ten fingers precisely so that we could say the rosary on our own hands.

Beads are nice, and I have quite a few rosaries I've collected over the years which mean a lot to me, but I find this little private practice of mine a good one, because it reminds me that the rosary is not really about the beads. I mean, the beads are just there to facilitate the praying. Our attachment to the things and objects of this world, even objects of prayer, isn't really the point, is it? Praying the ten-finger rosary is a way of voluntary simplicity, using just what God has given us, without a lot of ceremony. I think it is good to be respectful and all, but beads themselves don't mean anything in and of themselves. It's the rosary prayers that really matter.

Mother of God...

The image of garden, firmly at the heart of the rosary, indeed the very origin of the word itself, is not a static sign but rather a dynamic symbol. Symbols are many-faceted and multidimensional, indicating not one thing and one thing alone, but rather always pointing beyond itself to something that cannot ever be fully and completely known.

In the joyful time of Mary's early motherhood, the garden is a beautiful embrace, and the enclosure of the rosary offers similar protection and care, as well as the nurture of creativity and promise. But Mary is called to respond to the arc of her child's life, as Jesus becomes a grown man and inexorably moves into "greater knowledge of God's will and the courage to carry it out." Thus, in the sorrowful mysteries, Jesus enters quite a different kind of garden, a lonely awareness of who he is and what he must do that will separate him not only from conventional social and religious circles of his time but even from his own disciples and friends. The garden here has become Gethsemane, a place set apart, the solitary confinement of one's own unique, individual path. The conversation is no longer horizontal, the dialogue of mother and child in the lovely nursery garden of infancy. Instead, with mature awareness and complete surrender, the conversation is now undertaken in a vertical direction, between the chosen and the chooser, in the garden of consciousness.

Pray for us sinners now . . .

I've suffered repeatedly from depression throughout my life, and when it hits, it can be very baffling. Sometimes specific events trigger it, but many times it comes from nowhere and goes away for no apparent reason either. The bouts can last a day or a year, and until very recently, when I finally was able to get onto a medication that worked, all I really had was my meditation practice to help me through these depressions. I wasn't really into the rosary or a lot of the other traditional Catholic devotions, because most of my meditation training and workshops came more from Eastern-Asian traditions, concentrating largely on breath and body-consciousness. But after hearing a talk once at an East-West conference about the similarities between Christian meditative practices that use words like mantras to focus the mind, I realized that I didn't need to pay attention to every single word in prayers like the Hail Mary or the Jesus prayer. I could let the prayer flow over my mind, and when I did that, I was able to have the same kind of inner peace, the same relief from my inner turmoil and voices of self-hatred that I would often be able to have with breath-work or yoga.

So I do pray the rosary, but I don't use beads and I don't even say the words. My form of the rosary is entirely silent and mental, and I meditate on the mysteries by saying the prayers in my mind as often as I want until I feel like I'm done and want to move on to the next mystery. This form of prayer works for me by letting the spirit pray through me, I guess you could say. I like that I was able to find a part of my own religious tradition that I can relate to, after doing so much seeking in other traditions.

and at the hour of our death.

The winter and spring had been hard ones for me, as my father's health declined. Some days he would be better, then he'd have a hard time. About two or three times my sisters and I all thought that was it. All the rosary ladies at church were praying for me, so I felt well supported in prayer, but right after Christmas, it was clear from the doctors that Dad really only had a few days left. So as I prepared to go home, one of the women at church suggested to me that I go through my rosaries and choose one special rosary for the occasion of his death and to use that rosary throughout this whole period. I picked out a little hematite rosary that I had bought on vacation in Mexico with money my parents had given me.

I really thank my friend at church for this suggestion now, because that rosary has become so much more meaningful for me over time. There are many circumstances in which I feel my father has interceded for me in heaven, especially when it comes to family issues and conflicts. Holding that rosary for prayers

91

about those situations can sometimes be very hard for me, because it brings up sad and painful memories, and I miss him. But, as the priest said at his funeral, the sadness comes from how connected I am to him still, and the little black rosary I chose to accompany me has been very comforting.

Amen.

Second Sorrowful Mystery

Scourging

As soon as it was morning, the chief priests with the elder and the scribes and the whole council held a consultation, and they bound Jesus and led him away and delivered him to Pilate.... And again Pilate said to them, "Then what shall I do with the man whom you call the King of the Jews?" And they cried out again, "Crucify him." And Pilate said to them, "Why, what evil has he done?" But they shouted all the more, "Crucify him." So Pilate, wishing to satisfy the crowd, released for them Barabbas and having scourged Jesus, he delivered him to be crucified. (Mark 15:1, 12–15)

Hail, Mary . . .

In my devotion to the rosary, I cannot help but notice how uncomfortable the rosary seems to make liberal Catholics. On the Feast of the Holy Rosary itself as well as on other Marian feasts, I make it a point to go to the local Dominican parish, since in all probability at the usual liberal Catholic parishes where, admittedly, I do feel most comfortable attending, we might well skip over the feast entirely. I can always count on the Order of Preachers to put on a good solid, intelligent, insightful rosary celebration.

Since my conversion and subsequent confirmation in the Catholic Church — a process that came about directly because of my devotion to Mary through the rosary — this ambivalence has been my one big problem with liberal Catholicism. I cannot really see why a thirst for continued reform and *aggiornamento* cannot coexist with a devotion to the mother of Christ. It does in my own spirituality. There is no reason to continue to confine Mary to a plaster statue of 1950s femininity or to use her submission to justify sexist repression or to put her image forward as a latent argument for a restoration of divine monarchicalism. So while I am sympathetic to the liberal Catholic critiques of previous Marian pieties, the post–Vatican II period is one in which, despite all of the present pope's determination, the Mother seems to have been thrown out with the bathwater of preconciliar traditions and customs.

I am sad about this polarization I see around Mary, all the polite but intransigent liberal unease with her betraying an equally oppressive reactionary stiffness about her place in the divine hierarchy. Must we really scourge her image and meaning so thoroughly in the postconciliar Church? Can we not release her from the pillar where we have bound her by our own theological certainties and allow her to have her natural symbolic life in our imagination?

full of grace . . .

Small wonder I relish those Saturdays in ordinary time, when as a guest at the local Dominican community, where we have a "lady mass." (I miss it a little in Advent, but then, after all, the whole season is a big Mary festival, so I can't miss it too much). On these "ordinary" Saturdays, the Blessed Mother is made a special focus, the spoken prayers reflecting elements of her faith and love for Jesus, and we join our petitions to hers.

However, the best part is at the end. Before the just-smaller-than-lifesize wooden polychrome statue of Mary and baby

Jesus, her ivory-and-bronze rosary drawn in a graceful arc between her right hand and the child Jesus' left, we and the friars together sing one of the oldest and most beautiful Marian prayers, *Sub tuum presidium,* in a jaunty Latin chant that always raises my spirits.

"We take refuge in your protection, holy Mother of God. From the depth of our need, we ask you not to ignore our prayers but instead, O Blessed Virgin, always deliver us from every danger we might face!" The Gregorian setting always lingers sinuously on the last word *semper* in this chant, as if not wanting to end, and I find my meditations upon Christ's mother drawing my mind to the agelessness of generation upon generation of salvation history.

If Christ is yesterday, today, and forever, then his mother also is both now and forever. She is not a distraction or anachronism to me, and to feel her misunderstood and unrecognized is a source of religious pain for me. To know her, my Lover's mother, is for me a way into knowing and loving him more deeply. I don't know what people are so worried about when it comes to Marian devotion. As in the statue before which we sing, Mary does not push herself forward, but always stands behind Jesus, strong hip rocked gently forward so as to place him before her and before the whole world. To have him—and her—devalued, unrecognized, and misunderstood continues, to be a source of pain and conflict for me in my Church.

the Lord is with you.

Mary Gordon writes: "Her smells: lavender, ammonia, Pine Sol (always at the bottom of the commode), a green pool reminding you inevitably of the corruption that you, as a human being, had no right pretending you could rise above. Old lace, smelling of dust—hair oil, liniment. Unmodern smells that seem to us

Indian or pagan, rising from darkness punitive or curing: we could not tell which.

"The pictures on her walls were not about pleasing the eye. There was a brown picture with an imprint of Jesus' head: 'The Shroud of Turin.' Then the words to 'Now I Lay Me Down to Sleep' on a blue background, framed with an ivory border. A picture of Christ with long, smooth, girlish hair, pointing to his Sacred Heart, the size and shape of a pimiento or a tongue. Most mysterious: a picture made of slats. You turned your head one way: it was the Scourging at the Pillar. Another turn of the head produced Jesus Crowned with Thorns. If you looked absolutely straight ahead, you saw the Agony in the Garden. I spent hours looking at that picture, frightened, uncomprehending. It was part of my grandmother's hidden supernal path into the mystery of things, a hard road, unforgiving, made of beaten flesh."

Blessed are you among women . . .

Helen Sheehan, a former religious, writes: "I was told I had to conquer my pride and I tried to be humble, but no sooner did I make some advance than I took pride in my humility. This spirituality built around constant self-scrutiny and striving for perfection was torment to me, as it took my already extreme self-scrutinizing and perfectionist tendencies and turned them from constructive to destructive forces. It wasn't so much the self-scrutinizing and perfectionism that constituted the problem, as much as the fact that it was based on a dualism of body and spirit, of reason and faith, which went against the grain of my quest for wholeness. The anti-physicalism, and even more the anti-intellectualism, came as a constant assault on my character. Others simply let it roll off their backs without torturing themselves in the negative energy and the impossible contradictions that it engendered.

"We were gradually introduced to a whole series of secret practices: things which were never to be discussed outside the order, in fact, things which were not to be discussed inside the order, except to our superiors: examen, penances, acts of humility, chapter of faults and what was called the discipline.

"We knew nothing of the discipline until holy week. We were in retreat in preparation for the ceremony of being formally received into the order on Easter Monday. We had been immersed in the Good Friday liturgy, full of the vivid imagery of scourging at the pillar, bleeding from the wounds, carrying the cross, crucifixion, death for our sins. We then had a conference with the mistress of novices. She produced an instrument, a chain which branched out into a number of sub-chains, each with a hook at the end, and instructed us in the precise techniques of self-flagellation. Every Saturday night henceforth we were to go to the dormitory after night prayers and before recreation and remove our corsets (the stiff old-fashioned kind with stays and laces) and underpants and tie our stockings below our knees. No one who has never experienced it can know the sheer oddity of wearing layers upon layers of white linen and black serge and a long flowing veil and a stiff guimpe with no underpants making edifying conversation in the common room. At the end of recreation, the bell would ring, the lights would go out and the shades would go down. We pulled our veils down over our faces, our sleeves down over our hands, our skirts up over our backs. We would then take out our instrument and inflict it upon ourselves as hard as was possible without drawing blood, while reciting prayers in unison."

and blessed is the fruit of your womb, Jesus.

I remember the living room in our house on Lannon Street; hard-wood floors, two shaggy gray rugs, a couch and a chair or two, a fake fireplace, a piano, and one of the first one hundred TVs in the Midwest. We were a very religious family with statues and crucifixes and blessed candles, which we would light for protection against violent thunderstorms and tornadoes. My mother fondly carried the little pamphlet of prayers to Our Lady of Perpetual Help, whereas my dad habitually prayed the rosary. Not only would the beads of his regular rosary jingle in his pocket but he also had a tiny "ring rosary" on which he would count the ten Hail Marys as he was driving the car.

In those days, Bishop Sheen was very popular, and I attributed this saying to him, "A family that prays together, stays together." Well, that was gospel to my father. He would gather all seven of us and line us up around the perimeter of the living room. We each had our own set of beads. My brother and I were the youngest, probably six and four at the time. How I dreaded it — that long Apostles' Creed at the beginning; all the Hail Marys, over and over again; all those Our Fathers and Glory Bes. No one in my family knew what attention deficit hyperactivity disorder was back then, but I had it, and trying to stay with this monotonous ritual was torture. I remember looking around, wanting the words to go faster and faster and then finally be done. Kneeling throughout the twenty-five minutes was impossible, so I would often just scoot back on my haunches. A tiny glance from my mother would straighten me right back into prayerful position. One time, my dad had had enough with my shifting positions. He came right across that hardwood floor, picked me up and shook the living daylights out of me! The rosary, which had up to then been a sizeable annoyance, inspired in me a fierce loathing. Something inside me would strain and groan and push me to the edge. How I hated all that repetition!

What a surprise for my family and most people who knew me at the time to discover that I would feel called to join a convent!

Didn't they say rosaries in convents? Of course they did, and in my initial fervor, I tried to move into the so-called peace and meditation of the rosary, but as my mind was splintered in a million different directions, I didn't make much headway with this project: so much for the ability to shift internal mechanisms at will. To make things even worse, the nuns used the rosary as a form of punishment. If we "aspirants" (young women of high-school age aspiring to the vowed life) committed some heinous crime, for example, such as leaving our books on the study hall desks, we were made to say the rosary with outstretched arms at our midday prayer before lunch. So, there we were, lined up kneeling in the middle aisle of St. Dominic chapel with our arms raised, as if on the cross, rosary beads dangling down, repeating over and over again, "Pray for us sinners now and at the hour of our death." At the time, I could envision our deaths right then and there, leaving piles of expiring, rather than aspiring, young women on the chapel floor.

On other occasions, our directress, the sister in charge of a group of the young women, was a very light sleeper and she would jettison herself from her bed at the slightest noise. All three hundred pounds of her stomped upstairs, waking us all, as she demanded to know who had made the offending sound. No one came out from behind the quaking curtains which hung around our cells. Once my friend Patrice couldn't stand all the racket, so she simply told a lie and confessed to the crime, at which point she was promptly marched downstairs in order to — yes, you've guessed it — say the rosary with outstretched arms.

For these reasons, the rosary is more a source of resentment than means of grace for me, and yet, I can say there is probably something about the meditative repetition that soothes the soul. When my husband, Michael, was dying of cancer, there were nights when I couldn't hear him breathe. I would become silent, waiting to sense a movement or a slight breath from him.

He, too, was a light sleeper, and if I had moved over to try to listen better, he would have woken up.

So instead I simply began saying to myself a shortened form of the Buddhist loving-kindness meditation. There were three stanzas that I had memorized. The first was a prayer for myself which my anxious heart desperately needed:

> May I dwell in the heart.
> May I be free from suffering.
> May I be healed.
> May I be at peace.

The second quatrain flooded the bedroom with urgency:

> May you dwell in the heart.
> May you be free from suffering.
> May you be healed.
> May you be at peace.

The third and final piece opened the walls of our bedroom and brought to our wounded hearts every other suffering person in the universe:

> May all beings dwell in the heart.
> May all beings be free from suffering.
> May all beings be healed.
> May all beings be at peace.

Perhaps this is the rosary I was always called to say.

Holy Mary . . .

I do not gravitate naturally to the sorrowful mysteries. As much as I love the rosary for the regularity it gives to my inner life, the episodes of Jesus' Passion have been a challenge for me. When John Paul II announced that he was going to be recommending a new set of rosary mysteries focused on Jesus' ministry, I thought to myself, "Oh, perfect. I'll just say those mysteries instead of the sorrowful ones." Maybe I have seen too many bloody Spanish crucifixes in my lifetime, or maybe I have lived such a life of blessing that the kind of agony and physical suffering represented by the story of the Passion is difficult for me to relate to. I have the same problem with the story of Job, which seems to me like a Grimms fairy tale, unnecessarily mean-spirited and not especially enlightening at the end. I have long cringed at those graphic stories of martyrdom we hear sometimes, saints being grilled, ground up by lion's teeth, torn apart by tigers, dismembered. Physical torture is not inspiring or edifying to me.

So, I have had to back into mysteries like the Scourging at the Pillar. For me, what I have managed to come up with that makes sense and helps me is that the scourging represents the necessity we all face at some point in our lives to surrender to the inevitable. Having never been whipped or beaten physically, I cannot get into the literal image at all, but I do know how painful it is to realize that certain situations just simply must be endured because there is nothing to do about them. I cannot do anything about my aging, for instance. I cannot do anything about changing other people's obnoxious personality styles. I cannot be someone other than who I am sometimes—judgmental, fussy, self-centered. These are the sorts of things in my life that give me pain and that cannot be changed. So that's what I pray over, that I may receive the grace and wisdom to surrender and endure what cannot be changed.

Mother of God . . .

Having had both personal and professional contact with the workings of the criminal justice system, I see how easy it is to scapegoat someone outside of societal norms, to hide behind

101

the law in order to avoid a deeper and more painful examination of our individual brokenness and the causes of violence.
That's the story of Jesus' trial, conviction, and execution for me:
we take an innocent person, Jesus, who did nothing other than
reach out to touch, heal and love others, and we put him to death
to make ourselves feel better.

I'm not putting myself above this kind of scapegoating, because I do it as well. It is so much easier to say, "They are
the problem," than to really do an in-depth examination of
conscience: how have I treated someone unfairly? How am I
prejudiced or biased? Where is my own racism, homophobia,
classism? Can I let that rich person be compassionate without
discounting it? Can I let that drug-abusing brother-in-law of
mine hold an aspect of the wonder of God for me?

It is not fashionable in modern America to be engaged in an
active process of true repentance. There can be a lot of media-
driven breast-beating, but all of that is just more self-pity, in
my opinion, a way to get negative attention, like a neglected
teenager acting out. The challenge to engage regularly in a real
examination of conscience is one part of my Catholic faith that
I feel very grateful for, even if most people think I'm kind of
crazy when I say to them that I like going to confession. I don't
like it because it is fun but because in the end I feel purged,
like I've bled the sin out of me. I feel different, changed. My
pride is broken down, and I'm more open, more accepting, less
blaming.

pray for us sinners now . . .

I cannot really say when or even why I got into the phone-sex
habit, but at a certain point, I realized that it was no longer in my
control and that was the part that was scary. Because I talked to
my various therapists about it (never to my friends and never to

a priest), I did gain a certain kind of insight about the pattern and from there even learned a kind of compassion for myself. After all, most of my work was spent alone in the office, since the other two primary managers were usually out traveling around, and the vast majority of business I had to conduct was usually over the phone and by fax. So, really, some weeks I literally saw no one in the course of the work week and with virtually no oversight. It was pretty easy to simply call up one of those numbers, give them my credit card number, and spend some time at the end of the day by having phone-sex.

Of course, like my most addicts, I had a whole set of rationalizations for why it was okay to do this: it didn't cost very much, relative to my income; it was fun and completely safe, because after all I was never going to get infected over the phone, the way I had always been afraid might happen by accident with massage parlors; and by the time I was done, I felt relaxed and happy, so what was the harm? And then there was always the excuse that having given up alcohol and pot, I deserved a little harmless fun.

I can say that I never really, deep down, felt truly okay about it, in large part because of my pious upbringing, which I had very intentionally put behind me. When I went to church now and then, I could put the phone-sex out of my mind somewhat. However, the habit began to grow, and what initially was a twice-a-week kind of thing soon became a regular occurrence. If I didn't have privacy at the office, because one of the managers was there working late, I began to make the calls from home after rushing out in the middle of traffic thinking about nothing else, nothing but getting on the phone and having some fun, getting some relief. Soon it was a daily occurrence which got very expensive. Some months I was spending two or three hundred dollars on phone charges. Some nights I would spend hours, purposely delaying the end of the phone call, not to wanting to hang up until I eventually entered what I can only call an altered state, a kind of sex trance.

I knew about Twelve-Step programs for sex addiction, having gone to both Alcoholics Anonymous and Narcotics Anonymous earlier in my life, but for some reason, I couldn't really see this phone-sex pattern as an addiction. I didn't feel in control of it, but by the same token, it really wasn't all that destructive — just a kind of waste of time and energy. And I could afford the time, energy, and even the money it was costing me.

So one day, I was driving home from work, going a different route than the one I usually take because of traffic construction, and I drove past a church. At the same moment I went past, I saw a Filipino man on a bike, and when he passed by the front door, he crossed himself. The gesture startled me at the time, but it also brought up a lot of deeply buried memories of the old-world Catholic piety I grew up with. I had aunts who crossed themselves when passing churches, cemeteries, and other holy places, and that evening, this completely random gesture by a person I didn't know made me wake up: here I was, rushing to get home to dial up a sex service, and that's all I could think of. Wasn't that sad, I thought to myself, wasn't that pathetic, that that is what my life had come to.

So I pulled over, some force drawing me into this church. I had never been in this church before, and in our city, I expected that it would probably be locked, but to my surprise it wasn't. So I walked in. It was pretty dark that late afternoon in winter, and there was all the usual statues and things, but way over in the corner I saw a bank of red candles and I felt drawn to a large icon of Our Lady of Perpetual Help. I don't really know what made me do any of this, even today I don't know, but I lit a candle, knelt down right on the floor in front of the shrine, and started saying the rosary. It was like something from my childhood just came up inside me. I hadn't said the rosary in many, many years. I don't even think I owned a rosary at the time, but there I was, like one of my pious aunts, kneeling before the Blessed Virgin, asking her to help me. I didn't even know at the time what I was asking her to help me with. Remember, I didn't think I had a problem.

Anyway, I don't really know how much time passed. I could not have fallen asleep because when I came out of the meditative state, I was still kneeling, but all I can say is that I went somewhere else. I don't know where I went, but it was like I lost myself in the rosary, and I could really feel Mary's presence with me. She was very loving but also very retiring, very gentle. It wasn't dramatic at all. It was just like I woke up from a good solid sleep. I got up and went home, and when I went to pick up the phone, I really didn't want to disrupt the feeling of peace. It almost seemed to me that all the phone-sex stuff was from someone else's life. It just didn't even feel like me.

From that day on, I started going to that little chapel every day after work, praying five decades of the rosary on a little plastic rosary that the parish's rosary group had pinned to the bulletin board out in the vestibule for common use. After about a month, probably when my credit card bill arrived, I realized that I hadn't called any of those services. I'm telling the truth when I say that it never occurred to me to call them. It was like the whole burden of my loneliness and desperation had been lifted without my even asking for it. It feels a little melodramatic to call it a healing, but I do believe the Blessed Virgin removed this scourge from me when I prayed before her image and let the rosary prayer take the place of my own self-will.

and at the hour of our death.

I knew when I agreed to participate in the living rosary Brother Thich was organizing that I would be asked to meditate upon a sorrowful mystery. The idea was that we would be signed up with fourteen others to constitute a full fifteen-decade rosary, each of us committing for the rest of our lives to say a single decade on a mystery that we would be given. When, as we usually do after morning prayer, my friend Mary and I met for coffee, I said to her, "My spirituality is just not penitential or ascetic enough. I'm always eager to meditate on the joyful and the glorious, so I just know I'm going to get a sorrowful mystery to meditate upon for every day of the rest of my life. I just know it."

Sure enough, that evening at Mass, Brother Thich gave me my mystery — the Scourging at the Pillar. It probably wasn't all that appropriate to laugh, but that's what I did, and I showed the little slip of paper to Mary, as if she were my third-grade desk mate at parochial school. Now, most of the friars in formation are pretty sober, self-contained, thoughtful fellows, since the whole process of formation is pretty demanding for them. So there doesn't tend to be a lot of levity around the house or in the chapel — at least levity that we, lay people, see. Afraid that my laughter might be misunderstood, I explained quickly to the brother what my reaction was about. Not being all that downcast in my faith and aware of many blessings, I figured I would get a corrective mystery to balance things out, and as it turned out, I did. I waved the little piece of paper as punctuation

He looked up at me for a moment, making sure he understood my English, I think, and then he smiled slightly and touched my hand. "So...," he said warmly, his words inflected with his gracious French-Vietnamese accent, "When you have troubles, you give them to Christ. Think of him and let him carry them for you."

Amen.

Crown of Thorns

And they clothed him in a purple cloak, and plaiting a crown of thorns they put it on him. And they began to salute him, "Hail, King of the Jews!" And they struck his head with a reed, and spat upon him, and they knelt down in homage to him."
(Mark 15:17–19)

Hail, Mary . . .

Toward the end of the afternoon, after resting some and doing some silent meditation, I can feel the heaviness of the evening bear down some as I get dressed in the only allowable colors — tan, white, and black — trying within that range not to look too clerical, reminding myself to empty my pockets of everything but driver's license and car keys. "Nothing in, nothing out" is the primary rule at the prison and I imagine if I went more often than monthly, all of this would become routine. But it isn't quite yet for me, and all the small things remind me of what the evening will probably hold — pain, self-consciousness and regret, alongside hope, renewal, and even a strange joy in living.

I have made it a practice since the first night I was there to say the rosary on the way over and back, and I do so this evening as well. I was and still am sure it was the right thing for me to be doing, but having never been in a prison, having never been in any kind of prison ministry, I had no idea what to expect and my anxiety was riding high. Would it be like the lurid depictions of prison life shown on TV and in movies? I doubted that, even though some parts of my orientation had given me a bit of chill. For example, the "no hostage" policy made me think twice; if I were taken hostage, there would be no official negotiation for my release. Not to mention the various weapons I was shown that had been made from innocuous materials like newspaper and toothbrushes by prisoners with nothing but time on their hands. So it was not going to be a walk at the beach, but what would it really be like?

Looking back on that night, I always smile a little at the extent of my fear. After all, besides my own relative inexperience, San Quentin had a symbolic, almost mythic presence to it, sitting in one of the most spectacular locations on San Francisco Bay with over a hundred years of history. So, after e-mailing every single person on the planet that I knew to pray for me that first evening, what better to do than to take my little single-decade car rosary in hand and begin to surrender all my anxiety to the Lord and his Blessed Mother?

The trip over is just long enough to meditate upon the Joyful and the Sorrowful Mysteries, which prepares me excellently for what I call "the opposites" of the place. The prisoners we see at the chapel are interested in spiritual growth; most of them have a deep and abiding desire to know the Lord and already have prayer lives of a depth to be envied. The regularity, the monotony, and the expectation of constant obedience required of them all in prison is in more than one way like the life of a vowed religious community, and the effect is not lost on the men I see for individual direction. So every visit faces me with a contradiction that I must hold together: here in what many would probably call the worst place in the world, I regularly encounter sanctity, and far from discouraged, I feel myself privileged to be able to accompany individuals who know in their own lives the suffering and redemption that Christ knew.

I don't remember when I noticed the presence of greenery there beside the door to the prison chapel. It was probably — appropriately — around about the beginning of Lent, near the middle of my first year of volunteering, when one of my directees transformed the various garden patches around the courtyard into beautiful beds of many colors. So, while I waited for the guys to gather for the meditation group, I was probably especially focused that spring night on the plants, the roses and impatiens, the tall purple hollyhocks and fragrant masses of herbs coming into their own. About to go in and begin my session, I looked down and there, next to the door of the chapel, behind a little bush, I spied the stalks of a single crown-of-thorns branching out, vicious spines bristling all along the length of its snaky branches and at the very end, a bright red spot, a blood-red flower turned up to the sky. Here, too, were the opposites, violence and beauty, growth and defensiveness, and in my fantasy I imagined that it was a prisoner who planted it there, in all likelihood some years ago, judging by the size of it. Where was he now, I wondered to myself. Where was he now?

full of grace...

Each mystery contains the possibility of a particular grace and presents the situation in Jesus' life with his mother, in which he incarnated and lived that grace as an example to us. Living a life of faith, we are so often called to do things that we know in our heart of hearts are the right things to do, but which are hard to do, perhaps because of the situation or because of our own weakness or attachments. That's what the crown of thorns is to me — doing the right thing when it is hard, enduring the suffering, knowing it's part of the call to wholeness.

Being with my mother as she died was like that for me — very difficult on an emotional level because she and I didn't have a good relationship, and yet I knew I needed to be there. Almost as hard for me were the two times I needed to put my dogs to sleep—here they were, these beloved little beings whom I raised from puppies and, though I was just not going to let them go out of this world without me there, I can say that every fiber of my being resisted being a witness. Or my first gay parade. I knew I needed to be there, to be public, to show people that these are really living people that are being beaten up and abused and discriminated against, and yet I was very nervous about it. What would people think? Would I be on national television? But I knew it was right, to witness against hatred.

These are the more dramatic times, but there are all the little times, too — when you have to say something hard to someone you love, for the health of the relationship or for their own good: "I think you have a drinking problem," or "No, I'm not going to be able to lend you that money," or even, "You know, you really hurt me when you do that." Saying the rosary and especially meditating about the crown of thorns before I have to do the right, hard thing I'm being called to do is my way of preparing myself, putting it in God's hands, letting the Spirit act through me, asking for the moral courage to hold my head up and endure whatever is necessary. That's how Christ helps me through the rosary, by providing me an example of how to be strong and vulnerable at the same time.

the Lord is with you.

Crowns convey majesty and power to most humans, but a crown of thorns? When I visualize the Son of God with a crown of thorns pushed into his head, I think of the suffering and oppression brought by so many who wear the crown of authority, the false pride and vanity that too often accompanies the powerful. What a horrible way for the savior of the world to win our salvation: Jesus, naked, nailed to a cross, Jesus never complaining, Jesus, pardoning his executioners, Jesus letting Dismas the thief into heaven. Compassionate, loving Jesus. So I place my cares and troubles, my thorns, at the foot of the cross. Yes, I nail them there.

Blessed are you among women...

Yet another aspect of rosary-making is how small everything is. With exception of a few large pieces I have made, for statues or as habit-rosaries, mostly rosary-making is about dealing with the small, the delicate, the easily overlooked. Rosary-making is not dramatic or heroic.

In a society and culture in which bigger is better and louder is getting louder all the time, I take a kind of perverse, anachronistic delight in the smallness of my craft. I wonder if any of the people who now have my rosaries even notice some of their itsy-bitsy subtleties — how I've varied the colors on the miniscule spacers to create a background pattern, how I've inserted an unusual bead at regular intervals through the sequence as a kind of personal signature, that I've matched slight variations in the tone of some of the glass pieces so as to create a symmetry.

All of such attention to detail might well flirt with a kind of aestheticizing preciosity and thus undermine the spirituality of the rosary-making itself, but most of the times it's possible to stay on the right side of the line, because in the end, how grand can rosary-making really get? None of us are ever going to have a best-selling line of rosaries sold in only the best department stores nationwide, nor are we ever going to have international franchises or be featured in the pages of *Vogue*. The craft is by nature small and unassuming, a perfect example of Ste. Thérèse of Lisieux's "little way." We rosary-makers have our own experience of what she meant when she said, "I prefer the monotony

111

of obscure sacrifice to all ecstasies. To pick up a pin for love can convert a soul." We rosary-makers, however, might say it a bit differently: we prefer the monotony of obscure bead-stringing to all ecstasies.

Behind all of this aspect of the craft is the example of Christ's own smallness, his own humility. He did not deem equality with God something to be grasped at but instead set his soul in silence and peace. I aspire to the same in my rosary-making, to a simplicity and peace that discloses the divine to those who can see it.

and blessed is the fruit of your womb, Jesus.

I regularly use the mystery of Christ being crowned with thorns to meditate upon those important issues in my faith life around which I feel my conscience is still being formed (informed? transformed? reformed?). And right up there among the thorniest of issues is abortion. Until my conversion to Catholicism, this question was one I could largely sidestep. Being a gay man, I was unlikely to have to make the decision myself as to whether or not to terminate a pregnancy, and as a counselor, with perhaps two or three exceptions over the course of my practice, the women I saw had their own minds made up about the issue. However, having converted, having stood up and said, "I believe in all the holy Catholic Church believes, professes and teaches to be revealed by God," I cannot really in good conscience sidestep the issue or rationalize it away. So I bring the question again and again to the Blessed Mother in my prayer.

Abortion is indeed very much like a crown of thorns. There is nowhere to grasp it without getting stuck, and so it continues to sit, painful and unresolved, at least for me. And the thorns stick out in all directions. By grace, I have made some progress in resolution, but I am indeed still a far way away from being at peace. Both consistency and common sense lead me to see the unborn child as a living being, sacred, an expression of the Divine, and that the termination of a pregnancy is thus the termination of a life. On that much I am clear, and in that sense I find myself in good conscience able to affirm the characterization of abortion as a "great evil," however no greater an evil than any other willful termination of a life: homicide, suicide, capital punishment, war, the burning of heretics at the stake. Thus the relentless focus on the evil of abortion among my fellow Church members who don't seem particularly exercised over the other ways in which the sacredness of each human life fails to be upheld, pricks my conscience in another way. Such black-and-white thinking seems to me to be a way of avoiding the crown of thorns.

Which is the crux of the matter for me. Once I affirm all human life as sacred, I'm in the brier patch. I cannot imagine what good could possibly come from criminalizing abortion by making it illegal and subject to penalties: while the force of law would provide protection against violence, it cannot lead to a genuine conversion from violence. Moreover, such criminalization is inimical to how Christ himself is portrayed in the Gospels: he did not call upon the authorities to bring in the kingdom but rather brought each person to awareness of their own participation in the divinity of creation. And yet, in a broken, unredeemed world, we do as a society use the force of law to forbid individuals to take the life of other human beings, and those prohibitions — against murder, against suicide — flow directly from a respect for human life. Nor does it seem quite right, in our pluralistic society, to expect individuals who come from completely different religious, moral, and social traditions to hew to the Catholic line. Whether or not I myself agree with the point that it is birth, not conception, which brings a human being into the community, I know many individuals who indeed feel that way, very authentically and genuinely.

I also know many women who have had abortions who are clearly at peace in their heart of hearts with that decision, but I also know women who have not found that peace and for whom the abortion they decided upon troubles them greatly. Is it a matter of individual choice, in essence a pastoral matter, to be decided person by person, circumstance by circumstance? One resolution I can imagine is that the Church remove itself from political and legal advocacy and concentrate more fully on getting across to people the sacredness of all human life: in essence, seek to convert hearts through pastoral ministry, catechism, and the sacraments. And yet to sidestep the social and political ramifications of such an essential moral position in this way likewise smacks of trying to avoid wearing the crown of thorns.

Outside of conversations with my spiritual director, I have found no place to have a genuine and thorough discussion of the issue, and this, too, pains me. Over the years, before and after my conversion, I have expressed my questions on both the pro and the con side of the debate, hoping perhaps to have some dialogue, and every time, the discussion became immediately polarized, idiotically simplistic and fraught with attack and counterattack. To question the implications of Church teaching is to be accused of faithlessness. To affirm Church teaching gets one characterized as a mindless minion of a sexist and authoritarian institution. To leave the sweeping moral judgments up to the theologians and lower my sights to the pastoral level, choosing to address the issue as one of conversion rather than policy, is to be attacked for sneakily attempting to rationalize a lack of wholehearted assent to the magisterium. Yet, to make judgments about the rightness or wrongness of other people's actions concerning an agonizing situation that I myself have not had nor will ever have to face personally is to lay myself open – perhaps appropriately – to the charge of being judgmental and lacking true compassion.

So, like Christ – condemned if he did, condemned if he didn't – I continue to wear the thorny crown of conscientious unresolution, bringing abortion along with all the other moral issues I struggle with, to the lap of the Blessed Mother in prayer. If she cannot remove my suffering, at least I can have her with me as a witness, as a loving, encouraging presence, in a way that other fellow human beings cannot seem to be around such issues. In the absence of a fully formed conscience about such things, all I feel I can really do is continue to pray.

Holy Mary...

All my life I have attended Catholic school, and, to be honest, I cannot remember ever being taught about the history of the rosary. In fact, for as long as I can remember, I have been saying the Hail Mary prayer, and it has become so routine that I never really think about what I am actually saying. It just comes out. Even when I was being taught the prayer, I know that I was not truly learning the meaning of the words. I was just memorizing them because it was something we had to do. I think that is the problem with a lot of people. They do not really listen to the words coming out of their mouths. Part of that problem is probably because they do not know what the words they are saying actually mean. So I did some reading about the history of the rosary, which led me to think about the prayer more deeply, and once I had really picked apart the whole prayer sentence by sentence, I had a new appreciation for it.

Prayers are not just words. If you honestly believe in what you are saying, your prayers can change the world. With the rosary, we actively move our hands along the beads, which keeps our minds from drifting, helps us keep our focus, helps us picture in our mind the words we are speaking. The Hail Mary is so grammatically simple, such easy words, but the meaning behind every single word in the prayer is so powerful.

With my education in the rosary, I see that the power of the prayerful word goes back to the origin of the rosary itself. During the time of St. Dominic, there were holy wars breaking out that troubled him deeply. Dominic decided that instead of using actual weapons and a means to fight, he would use prayers. As he said to the soldiers at that time: "You will not change the way of your enemies by killing them. Pray for them. God alone can make them better men." Hard words to understand, especially for soldiers, but soon they realized what he was saying: prayers, not war, can truly change the world.

Mother of God . . .

Webster defines "weapon" as "an instrument of any kind used for fighting. Any means of attack or defense," and most interesting, the example in my dictionary illustrates this use of the word with the sentence: "his best weapon was silence." Think about Jesus before Pilate and how Jesus used the weapon of silence in responding to Pilate, his love absorbing evil, the healer himself as the battleground.

The weapons of hate, destruction, and violence can never bring us peace, but the weapon of love can conquer evil, for evil loses its power in the presence of love. In this way, the rosary is a weapon, an instrument used to defend, God's own power in our hands, invoked to destroy whatever holds us in bondage to sin and evil.

How many times there have been when I have either been tempted to sin or have been in a dangerous situation, praying the rosary has literally led me out of the temptation or kept me safe. It has been a weapon of love for me, by defending me and defeating the power of temptation. The graces I have received in these situations I attribute to the power of the rosary.

pray for us sinners now . . .

Have you noticed that even mortification can be a strange kind of pleasure in religious life, defeating its purpose of fostering detachment, surrender, and patience? My own piety grew up within a very Italian atmosphere — ornate, sensual, the proverbial "smells and bells" of just barely before Vatican II — and so I feel very much at home in those vaulted places, crammed full of statues and candles, every inch of stone carved, every piece of wood painted. However, when my spiritual life deepened and I had my contemplative opening — due in large part to the rosary — I suddenly discovered that much of what I had previously considered to be prayer was actually distraction. It was me, talking to myself in my own head about what I was perceiving, feeling, liking, wanting.

The rosary with all its tedious repetitions managed, in a very marvelous and unexpected way, to mortify this perceiving mind of mine, to distract me from my distractions, so to speak, and in doing so, I became aware of the utter simplicity, the unity, the sheer spare beauty behind everything I could see with my eyes. It is indeed all one, this world of ours, this beautiful creation, all one in its being, despite all the multiplicity of forms, despite the sensual pleasure offered by the colors, the fragrances, the shapes. Contemplative prayer thus became for me a time set aside for me to practice this kind of second-sight, to see beyond what "appears" so as to get a direct, unmediated sense of what "is," in its "is-ness" as Meister Eckhart would put it. I turn away from the varied individual beings around me and move into conscious relationship to the "being" itself, the source of being. As I am continually reminded by the wise people around me who give me spiritual direction, the rosary is at the most basic level a contemplative practice.

So for a time I swept away all the ornamentation of my spiritual life and let myself be drawn to a spare, monastic piety. I made it a practice to go to Mass or on retreat at some of the hospitable local religious communities, whose commitment to a contemplative way of life manifested itself in large, empty, silent spaces in which to pray or adore the Sacrament, a studied, careful simplicity in dress, in décor, in food. It was a good thing for me, a healthy compensation, to train myself away from all the elaboration, to let my mind, my eye, my senses rest in the quiet and the emptiness. And for a while, I fooled myself into thinking that this was mortification of the senses: to sit motionless in the huge void of the Camaldolese chapel at Big Sur, with nothing but an enormous undecorated block of an altar beneath a severe iron crucifix hung from the ocular window; to shiver in the concrete immensity of the sanctuary of Newman Hall, high, wide, and empty, its two shrines to Our Lady pushed out to the corners of the space, out of sight; to sit in the sheer blackness of night at St. Albert's before dawn, before morning prayer, unable to see or hear anything but my own sleepy breathing.

Not until I happened upon the Perpetual Adoration chapel just before Christmas one year did I come to see how wrong I was. Saying the rosary before the exposed Eucharist had come to be a rich source of consolation for me, usually confined by time and practice to a half-hour with the Dominicans twice a week and then only once a year at my own parish's Forty-Hours devotion. By chance one day I came upon a flyer for a Perpetual Adoration run by the Divine Mercy Society of a local church, and I was quite happy. Here was a place I could go at any time and spend some quality contemplation time. The Spirit was at work!

Indeed, the Spirit was at work, but as usual, not in any way I expected. Expecting something akin to what I had been used to in recent years playing part-time monk, I walked into the Perpetual Adoration chapel to behold a place that in no way conformed to my idea of beautiful. The room itself was clearly converted from a leftover parish office — paneling from the 1960s tacked up on the walls, furnished with old gooseneck lamps, rickety folding chairs, and old cushions squished down to pancakes from years of use. The host was placed in a monstrance that looked like spray-painted rebar, illuminated neither by soft candlelight nor by a single, dramatic beam of overhead track lighting, but rather by a reading lamp that had been inexpertly twisted around to shine on the altar from the side. All about the chapel were statues and pictures of saints well within the decidedly lachrymose-sentimental tradition of popular piety. In short, nothing like the clean lines or gleaming simplicity at the retreat houses and other chapels I had been frequenting.

I could feel myself bristle and immediately could hear my mind begin to click off all the many judgments about this place. It was, to my eye, supremely ugly, inelegant in ways I couldn't have intentionally imagined, dowdy, outdated, unwealthy in both materials and creativity. And yet, there he was, my Lover, in the form of the consecrated Host, drawing me forward, inviting me to stay with him, to be with him, to pray with him awhile. So, while my aestheticism reeled in the face of all this tastelessness, my body automatically and spontaneously dropped down to the floor, kneeling and bowing, my forehead to the ground, my hands folded before me. He was here and I could feel him, and finally that was all that mattered.

In this fusty little chapel in El Cerrito, California, I came to know what a true mortification of the senses was. I had been fooled, tricked by my own gratification into thinking all the Zen-style elegance of monasticism was doing me any kind of spiritual good. Spartan those places were, indeed, but delightfully spartan, sensually pleasing, providing for me at least a completely different form of distraction – the distraction of congratulating myself on my own fine elegant taste for simplicity. This Eucharistic chapel, on the other hand, was true mortification: on no level did I enjoy what it looked like and instead its very dowdiness brought up and out of me my worst snobbishness.

What better thing to bring to Christ than this snobbishness and self-deception? What better offering to lay upon the altar? And what better practice than to pray the rosary in a place of discomfort and human weakness, to find a way to let all the judgments drop away and to see him, only him, in my mind and heart?

I go to this chapel often now, since it is on my way home from San Quentin prison where I do the volunteer spiritual direction, and every time I step inside, I cannot help but react in the way that I did that first time. But, by the grace of God, it doesn't last long. I make my obeisance before the Host, take out my rosary, and offer up all my petty suffering to Jesus, who knew both the beauty and ugliness of this world and who surrendered to it all as a manifestation of God's immensity.

and at the hour of our death.

Even though I pray the rosary quite often, it has become so much part of my life, that I say the words as if I were possessed, without really stopping and thinking about what they truly mean. I'm a little frustrated with myself about this, to tell the truth, because when I pray, I like it to mean something. Prayer shouldn't be just an ordinary, everyday habit. Prayer, in my way of thinking, is time to myself, the most special part of my day, something I can look forward to and know that it will heal my soul and ease my worries.

The rosary tells the story of our Lord, and in this story, I finally came to understand the real power Mary holds. I hadn't really fully understood why we prayed to her. I knew she was the Blessed Mother but never really thought about it, but through praying on the mystery of the Annunciation, reflecting on the angel Gabriel telling Mary, "You are the Mother of the Savior," it became evident to me that Mary is more than Jesus' earthly mother. Her special qualities become even more evident when I meditate upon the sorrows she endured later in her life with her son, the greatest pain of all for a mother, to see her own son scorned, bleeding, and dying. In these mysteries I see her true importance to us. We don't pray to Mary because she is another saint or someone that is supposed to help us in time of need. These are basic reasons but not genuine intentions. We pray to Mary because she has suffered and seen the worst of the world, and yet she still had faith. She still believed. In herself, she holds the superlative qualities of all mothers and healers. Behind every courageous child, like Jesus, we know there is an even more powerful and courageous mother, like Mary.

Amen.

Carrying the Cross

So Jesus came out, wearing the crown of thorns and the purple robe.... [And Pilate] said to Jesus, "Where are you from?" But Jesus gave no answer. Pilate therefore said to him, "You will not speak to me? Do you not know that I have the power to release you, and power to crucify you?" Jesus answered him, "You would have no power over me unless it had been given you from above...." So they took Jesus, and he went out, bearing his own cross to the place of a skull, which is called in Hebrew Golgotha. (John 19:5, 9–11, 17)

Hail, Mary . . .

Even Jesus fell under the weight of the cross. That's what I remind myself when I am praying for those poor souls I see on the street, the mentally ill, the homeless, those without anyone to pray for them. I think about what burdens they have carried, what situations they were born into, over which they had no control: alcoholic parents, war-torn countries, poverty, no educational possibilities. And here they are, broken under the weight of these crosses.

We don't really look at the faces of the homeless. I discovered this about myself when a few years back, I decided for a Lenten discipline to give money to whoever asked for it. Not a lot of money, just change or a dollar or two, but the discipline was to give to whoever asked and not worry about the result. That's when I realized that I had been passing by certain individuals literally for years without actually looking at them, never seen their faces, never knew the color of their eyes, how they looked when they smiled, who had a Southern accent and who came from New York. And the first day I did this, I barely made it home before bursting into tears, tears of remorse for my own hard-heartedness, tears of compassion for these individuals broken by the circumstances of their lives until they had only the streets and the kindness of strangers.

That's when the rosary mystery of Jesus carrying the cross came alive for me. So what I do now during the fourth sorrowful mystery is I call to mind the face of someone I know who has been broken by life. Sometimes it is a homeless person that came to my parish's soup-and-suppers. Or it could be someone I actually knew, like a friend of mine who lost his parents and never has really dealt with it, or even further back in my own past, the crazy lady that lived in the unkempt house that we kids refused to go to for trick-or-treat.

We don't pay attention to people like this. I know I don't. So I use the rosary to bring these people to mind, and I contemplate my beloved Jesus falling under the weight of the wood. Even he fell. Yes, even he fell under the weight of his mortal life.

full of grace...

The steps down from the entry led into a basement that had been remodeled, plastered a warm yellow and lit with sconces, into a showroom for the *retablos,* and the large dark Mission furniture had the effect of making me think I had stepped for a moment back into the nineteenth century, into the *sala* of some wealthy, pious landowner. Here hung the entire collection, many of the *retablos* I had seen in the catalogue and on the net, many, it appeared, new to me. These little squares of tin, hand-painted with such elegance and naïveté, were bewitching not just for their folk-art directness but because of their subjects for whom I felt such affection: St. Joseph, as a handsome young father holding a slumbering Christ-child, each with a lily in his hand, a few glorious Queens of Heaven bedecked in elaborate dark gowns, studded with gold and jewels; simple peasant Marys holding doves flying up to heaven from her immaculate heart; strange and slightly disturbing Trinities, Father, Son, and Holy Spirit as identical middle-aged men, sitting about a table conversing.

But then I turned a corner into the small room beside the main one and there, on my left, he looked at me from a faded *nicho,* eyes large and luminous, lips drawn, a diadem of blood sprinkled across his smooth forehead. This was a Man of Sorrow unlike others I had seen. This artist, following an Italian mannerist style reinterpreted for colonial Mexico, decided to paint a close-up of Christ's face, with only the tip of the massive cross he carried visible in the upper right of the frame.

His eyes held a question and without thinking, I whispered to him, "What do you want?" That silent, suffering look — was it imploring our compassion? Questioning the depth of human cruelty? Hoping we would remain faithful to what he had taught us?

It was a beautiful piece of work, more naturalistic than most of the genre and executed with superb smoothness of oil technique. And I could have afforded it. But in truth, I did not know if I could bear to see him day by day, his suffering so close to me, his eyes so deep with wonder and pain.

the Lord is with you.

Rosary-making requires yet another aspect of contemplative prayer I have discovered: concentration and persistence. There is no way I can really make rosaries with all these teeny-tiny little parts and tools and pieces and beads and so on without really concentrating. If I'm distracted, all of the stuff is going to go all over my kitchen, or worse, I'll have gotten to the end of stringing the beads only to find that I'm missing a bead or have one too many beads. By the way, this never happens at the end of the stringing — it is an unwritten law of the rosary-maker's universe that missing or extra beads will always occur in the middle decade of a five-decade rosary, so that the whole thing will need to be taken apart and put back together.

Concentration is key, so I make sure the TV is off, the day is uncluttered, the room is neat and clean, and that I'm not upset or angry or anxious or whatever. I have to let go of everything else in my mind and in my heart and really give myself over to the work. I hesitate to call this mortification — that sounds way too exalted — but it does require at the very least persistence.

Blessed are you among women . . .

Garry Wills writes: "One of our duties was to say the rosary every night after visiting hours. We knelt on a stair landing between floors, so anyone who wanted to join in could assemble on the floor above or the one below. A devout Protestant patient said he would never do such an idolatrous thing, the plain Bible was good enough for him, not any of this papistical stuff. I argued that the repeated Hail Marys of the rosary were made up, in large part of the gospel verses. . . . I think the man may have come to one rosary, but I did not convince him. Instead,

I convinced myself. The arguments still seem good to me, so I have maintained the lifelong habit of saying the rosary."

and blessed is the fruit of your womb, Jesus.

Over the years of praying the rosary, I have tended to use the rosary as a way to respond to situations that I don't know how to respond to in any other fashion. Some circumstances or problems, particularly on a social level, are almost insoluble to me, and certainly more complex for me to figure out on my own. So that's when I pray the rosary. I just hold the whole situation in my mind, and usually I pray the sorrowful mysteries.

My own parish is kind of modern-liberal, so there's not a whole lot of rosary-praying, no regular communal recitation before or after Mass. But there's a small group of us with a devotion to the Blessed Mother, more or less secret, I think, from most of the parishioners. When we got a flyer in the bulletin announcing that the city's Religious Witness with the Homeless would be mounting a large wall display in front of City Hall with the names of all the homeless who had died on the streets over the past twenty or so years, I turned to my friend Tom and said, "Hey, you want to go down tomorrow morning and pray the rosary?"

He smiled and answered laconically, as he tends to do, and said, "Sure. When?"

"How about 8 a.m.? Then you can get to work."

"Sure."

I sent out a little e-mail bulletin to the Peace and Social Justice group and to a few other parishioners I knew would be interested, some of whom spearheaded our parish's own ministry to the homeless youth in our neighborhood with supper and fellowship on Wednesday night. I didn't really know what the response would be to the idea of all of us getting together to stand around in public on a work day praying the rosary, but I knew that if the only people who came were me and Tom, the Blessed Mother would be listening.

About a dozen people showed up, and it was interesting for me to think that after being a member of the parish for a few years, this was really the first time I had ever prayed the rosary with any of my fellow parishioners. It felt really good. No one really honors the memory of these poor people who died right in front of our houses, churches, and businesses, and I stood there, praying the Hail Mary, wondering to myself who loved them, who missed them still. We regularly hear petitions in church on behalf of those "who have no one to pray for them," and surely this is a group of such people.

Our Peace and Social Justice group has formed itself around the idea of shared prayer, reflection, and discussion, and we occasionally hear from the more action-oriented in the parish a little dig or two about this contemplative orientation of ours. However, many of us have spent lots of time in doing direct service and charity, and, speaking only for myself, I feel not enough time is given to prayer and reflection over these issues.

What did we accomplish by standing there and praying in front of the names of strangers? Wouldn't it have been better to make sandwiches, give away money, provide health care? I'd like to think that praying the rosary was a way to accord these souls the dignity and respect they did not have in life. I felt a little bit like the Blessed Mother's representative there before the wall of the homeless dead, Mary who loves and weeps over all her children.

Holy Mary...

I have a very simple Black Madonna, painted like Our Lady of Guadalupe, that I bought from a local artist after seeing the piece displayed in, of all places, a Starbucks. I stopped in to get a quick coffee on the way to church, and there she was. It looked sort of old, like a tempera on wood, but I knew it was modern, and the artist herself seemed surprised at the strength of my devotion to the Blessed Mother. In fact, she didn't really know much about Mary from a Catholic perspective but had been very taken with the idea of the Black Madonna, so I guess the piece I have is part of a whole series.

I like praying the sorrowful mysteries in front of this piece in the afternoon, as the sunlight is dying, and the way she is painted, her body bent over a little and her little eyes looking up, is the way I envision Mary looking at her son as he carries the cross past her. Her face is so dark, all you can see are her eyes, and she looks so small and so vulnerable, like an uneducated peasant girl caught up in a situation too big for her to comprehend or handle.

The sorrowful mysteries depress me, and I sometimes have to skip them altogether, but with my Lupe I feel like I can get through them. I join my sorrow with hers, and she makes me want to take back the many crosses I have laid on the backs of other people with my impatience or my self-pity. Her figure is almost haunting, and I sometimes close my eyes and see her there, in her deep green robe, looking at her son go to his death. She puts everything in perspective for me.

Mother of God . . .

It is a little embarrassing, I think, to talk about using the rosary in this way. I'm sure some of my religion teachers would be mortified that I would consider being so presumptuous, but it was a very, very difficult period in my life. My own health was not good, my work life was very stressful, since my husband had been out of work for over two years. Up to that point, I was making sufficient money to support us, but it became clear that we were at the end of that time, and despite many good efforts on his part, each job seemed to fall through. I prayed daily, in fact, many times a day about this whole situation, mostly that I could maintain my own mental and physical health long enough to get us to the point where he was employed again, but also for him. The continued unemployment was really getting to his self-esteem, and the kind of jobs he was applying for were jobs that he really wanted, things he would feel really good doing, service-oriented positions in good organizations. So a lot of my prayers to the Virgin were that she intercede so that he could do good for others through his employment — I didn't want to be all selfish. Anyway, we both thought he had this one position sewn up, since the director of the program had actually called him and recruited him, and I fully expected that I would come home and he would have been hired and all my faith in prayer would be redeemed and everything would be perfect.

God had other plans. At the last minute, a person whose qualifications perfectly fit the job he was applying for got wind of the job and was hired by the agency, instead of my husband. I was totally crushed, and, frankly, I was very frustrated. I broke down in tears at first and then later, when my husband wasn't around, I raged. In fact, I yelled at God so hard that I was hoarse for three days. How could he not help my husband? How much more was I expected to bear? Why torment us both with such an excellent possibility and then yank it away? How dare this other person get the job when we needed it so badly? I am afraid to say, I was not especially kind, forbearing, or gracious that day, and in a fit of pique, I vowed that I was going to say nothing but the Sorrowful Mysteries every day until my husband got hired. It was the middle of the summer but I declared my own private Lent: from that August until he was hired in December, I said the Sorrowful Mysteries each and every day.

Eventually, thank God, my anger subsided, and to tell you the truth, I had never heard of anyone using the rosary of all things to express anger at God. After a while, it seemed a bit like holding a grudge, but on the level of my soul, I must tell you that it was comforting in a strange way. Of all the mysteries, the Sorrowful Mysteries had always been my least favorite. I'm a much more upbeat person who didn't grow up with a gloomy, dark Catholicism. But during that period, praying them day after day after day, I came to appreciate them: the experience of being humbled, of enduring pain, of putting one step in front of the other, carrying the cross, letting yourself be crucified again and again and again by life if that is your path. It was comforting because that part of Christ's life fit my experience. I felt him with me. I was brought to a deeper awareness of him through the Blessed Mother. I knew in my own little way the nature of suffering, suffering for another.

When my husband was hired, it was just before Christmas, and by then, I was more than ready to shift into Joyous Mysteries. It had been a very intense autumn, internally and externally, and a new liturgical year began. But since that time, I have sometimes taken up a single cycle of mysteries for an extended period of time, rather than cycle through them as I usually do. When the September 11 bombings happened, for example, I said the Sorrowful Mysteries for a whole month, in honor of the dead and the grieving. And during the formal Christmas season, I say only the Joyous Mysteries. The extended concentration on them day after day discloses new things to me, I find – like a rosary intensive rather than a survey course you might say. Or like a hologram, in which each piece of Christ's life contains the whole of Christ's life – the crucifixion has the nativity and the ascension in it, just as the Annunciation anticipates the scourging and the Assumption. It is all one, so sometimes I think it is good to just concentrate on a single set of mysteries and let the whole come forward from this small part. Anyway, it's worked for me.

pray for us sinners now . . .

I usually dedicate my rosary for a specific intention, but I don't usually ask for favors. One exception to this I can think of was a plane trip from Athens, Greece, to New York City. There was a terrible storm that forced the plane to land in Bangor, Maine, and the pilots, busy with the emergency, didn't inform the passengers of the reasons for the delay and route change. When we finally took off for New York and made the connection back home to San Francisco, we arrived in the early morning instead of the night before. I always called this the "three-rosary flight," since praying the rosary kept me calm, and, I'd like to think, added to whatever serenity there was in that hot, stuffy passenger cabin.

and at the hour of our death.

The cross is the juncture where we all meet, the crossroad of our faith. All Christian traditions come together here, and from here we all move out into different directions or paths. It is a stumbling block, as St. Paul says, and my meditations upon the cross over time have made the truth of his statement so much more clear to me with every passing year. The relationship to suffering that it represents distinguishes Christianity from all other religions: suffering is neither an illusion nor an aspect of the Divine. Suffering is how we experience our limitation as creatures in the face of the enormous, all-encompassing reality of eternal Being from which we have been separated. Thus by enduring suffering consciously, by choosing not to resist, by carrying the Cross, we are reminded of the way back, how to re-unite with the infinite. This is Jesus' singular spiritual insight which I believe led him to an awareness of his own substantial unity with God. The cross and his submission to its truth are the doorway into eternity for us as his followers. We refuse to take it up at our own peril. We shoulder its weight as he did, willingly, consciously, and we move ever closer to that place where all existence comes together, to that center marked by the intersection of all that is.

Amen.

Crucifixion

Standing by the cross of Jesus were his mother, and his mother's sister Mary the wife of Clopas, and Mary Magdalene. When Jesus saw his mother, and the disciple whom he loved standing near, he said to his mother, "Woman, behold you son!" Then he said to the disciple, "Behold, your mother!" And from that hour the disciple took her to his own home. After this Jesus, knowing that all was now finished, said (to fulfil the scripture) "I thirst...." When Jesus had received the vinegar, he said, "It is finished"; and he bowed his head and gave up his spirit. (John 19:25-28, 30)

Hail, Mary...

I have a particular rosary I use when I go to execution prayer vigils. It is made of large black onyx beads, with Our Fathers almost as big as children's marbles — very heavy, very masculine, very dark. The silver Mission-style crucifix on the end is quite thick, with its bottom shaped like a wedge, like a dagger, or a stake, or a signpost to be sunk into the ground. The figure of Christ is contorted and stylized so as to look almost pressed into the frame of the cross, his ribs crude, deep horizontal slashes, his palms black voids, with a head bowed so deeply that it seems to sink into his shoulders.

Nevertheless, his large eyes look out beneath his brow, look out at me as I hold the crucifix in the palm of my hand, and I have spent many hours looking back at him. I have said this rosary on the ground before the East Gate of San Quentin at night, as the noisy protest rally winds onward, Native American drumming, religious in habits holding hands and singing softly, while the guards walk back and forth looking impassive, sometimes disdainful, sometimes amused, sometimes wary. I have said this rosary quietly beside the Buddhist Peace Fellowship at sunrise in front of the Federal Building in Oakland, the crowd sparse, employees passing by us, averting their eyes, on the way to work, people drinking their lattes at Starbucks across the street, not listening to the bullhorn, not looking at the placards.

When I say an execution rosary looking into the eyes of the crucified one, I am beyond questions and answers. I pray with no other intention than to be with him and to be spiritually and emotionally present to the whole situation: to the violence that led us to this moment; to the violence being perpetrated in my name, to the guilt and innocence of all of us. If anyone can help me hold all the conflicting opposites together at this time, it is this heavy, dark, crucified Christ. Like Mary, I pray at the foot of the cross, torn and sorrowing, bereft of hope, hanging on to faith. This rosary has a terrible weight to it.

full of grace . . .

His eyes lit up when he heard that I repaired rosaries. "I bring you one and you repair, okay? It is the one my mother had in her hand when she died, but it is broken now and I want to use it. You can fix it, yes?"

I nodded and smiled. "That's what I do. Only I'm going to restring it on jewelry wire. That way it will be very strong and never come apart again."

He brought it the next week to Mass, wrapped in a little bit of plastic, the sacred circle broken in two places. There's something so sad about broken rosaries. At first I wasn't sure what the beads were — flat, kind of brownish, grayish red — but that afternoon, I laid out my dish towel and pliers, slowly took the tiny little chain apart, piece by piece, and prayed for his mother as I pieced the rosary back together, bead by bead by bead. I didn't know her, and indeed, I hardly knew her son, but I could feel her presence with me that day. It is an awesome thing to be working upon the last object in the world that someone touched before leaving this life, and in the end, I liked how the new rosary looked, still a bit olden-style and yet, clean, neat, complete.

He started crying a little when I gave it to him before Mass that next Sunday, and he immediately kissed it, which I thought was really sweet since I'm always kissing my rosaries, too. His friend next to him wondered aloud what the beads were, and I said, I couldn't really tell, I thought they might be plastic, but then his friend held the rosary for a moment, running a couple of them over his hands and peering at them really closely. *"Son semillas, sabes. Semillas,"* he said definitively. And I knew he was right. She had been holding a rosary of little seeds when she passed from this life into the next, and now her son was holding them, ready to pray.

the Lord is with you.

Arriving at my parish the afternoon of September 11, 2001, I found about fifteen people already sitting in silent prayer with the Reserved Host on the altar table. After several minutes of contemplation, I took out my rosary beads not knowing how I would pray. So, I chose the rosary because Mary, the mother of God Incarnate, had lived her life amid faithful questioning

135

and obedience, fearing for her son's safety, and surviving the tragedy of his crucifixion. As I began each decade, I asked, "How is the Gospel revealed in today's horrible events?" In the following order came five answers:

1. Death comes like a thief in the night.

2. Death is personal and individual. Each person who died, terrorist and victim, was loved by a family or friends, and by God.

3. Jesus taught that love is the way of God, not power. He refused political or military leadership as the stuff of humanity, not divinity.

4. How quickly I can abandon Christian love in favor of revenge, violent retribution, including war? This response surprised me into thinking about the power of evil in human motives.

5. God's mercy is undiminished and everlasting. Life can go on, even in sadness. There were background noises of children playing in the school yard, laughing and yelling to each other, while grownups were sitting in stunned silence trying to understand the nature of the tragedies we witnessed that morning.

Blessed are you among women...

Every rosary is a paradox, which is a kind of a cross—two opposite things intersecting. Like crosses, every one is the same, but each one is different. That's how it is with rosaries, the same insight that a friend of mine came up with one day, after she became quite taken with the rosaries I was making. Her image was less grim and more poetic. She said that rosaries were fascinating because they were like sonnets: in paradoxical fashion, the strict conventions of the traditional form nevertheless permitted myriad individual variations within that form, so that every sonnet was simultaneously like and unlike every other sonnet. The same basic format and conventions allow every rosary their own individualities, their own histories for the individuals who pray with them, their own individual meanings and purposes.

This bit of wisdom about rosaries is what I believe in my heart of hearts about people: within the same basic form and conventions — two hands, ten fingers, propensity to love and to hate, a tendency to form societies and cultures — we each have our own amazing individuality. Rosaries are perfect symbols for the paradox of unity and diversity in God's creation — at the most basic level we are one, and yet not one of us is like any other.

I also think this is true about the crosses of suffering we each carry. Each one of us certainly suffers alone, but because everyone suffers, none of us really suffers alone. Christ himself dies, but in his death he carries the sorrow of the whole world, in a heart of infinite compassion, suffering with us all, for us all. This paradox of community and individuality is the paradox of the cross, and my rosary-making has helped me to appreciate its truth.

and blessed is the fruit of your womb, Jesus.

I did not see my mother open that drawer very often. In her top left-hand dresser drawer, she kept her rosary. I am not a son who can recount stories of my family praying the rosary together after dinner every evening. We were not that kind of family. My mother is a cradle Catholic, but a very sensible, practical one, who tries her best to live her faith and to practice Christian principles in all she does. She taught my brother and me the same principles, quietly and by example. My father converted to Catholicism at the age of thirty, and, though he is probably more devout in his faith than any of the rest of us, he does not pray the rosary daily either.

The only time I ever saw my mother open that drawer and take out the rosary was when she was attending a wake or vigil, as we now call it, for someone she knew who had died. Very often, even from an early age, I would attend with her, and it was these experiences that taught me about the rosary, its devotion, and the fifteen mysteries that were contemplated. To my knowledge, this was the only rosary my mother ever had up to that point in her life. The beads were well worn after all those many wakes over the years.

Years later, after I had finished graduate school, my older brother and my only sibling died in a drowning accident up in the northern desert of California, where he had just moved his family after accepting a job promotion. He was only thirty years old at the time. Within less than twenty-four hours, our family gathered to be with his wife and two small children and to make arrangements for his funeral and burial to take place back in the Bay Area where we grew up. Before we drove home, my parents and I stopped at the local funeral home to collect my brother's personal effects and then we continued our long journey back to prepare ourselves physically, emotionally, and spiritually for his scheduled obsequies.

A couple of days later, it was time to go to our hometown funeral parlor, to view his body for the first time since his death. None of us had seen him dead, and to tell the honest truth, I think secretly each of us wanted to believe that when we did open the casket there would be someone else. We were still so profoundly in shock at the accidental and unexpected death of this healthy man at such a young age. My mother did not want to go to the viewing, preferring to remember her first-born son alive and full of vigor, so my sister-in-law, my father, and I volunteered for the difficult task.

If my memory serves me correctly, three o'clock was the time we were due to be there, and so my father and I left the house about twenty minutes early to pick up my sister-in-law. Almost out the door, I heard my mother call me back. "Would you please do me a favor?" she asked. "Of course," was my reply.

I followed her into the bedroom and watched her carefully open the top left-hand drawer of her dresser and remove her rosary. It had been so many years since I had seen her retrieve it that I had almost forgotten that it was there. As she pressed the beads into my hands, she asked that when my brother's casket was opened for the viewing, that I place her rosary in his hands, rather than the one the mortuary would have normally provided. It was a mother's final request before her son would be placed in the ground.

Not many people know this story, but it was my privilege to carry out my mother's request, in the same manner she tries to live her faith — quietly, with dignity, and without fanfare. The rosary my brother was given, the last gift on this earth from his mother, seems to me to be a very fitting symbol of her faith, a faith buried with him and which accompanies him now after death.

Holy Mary

The Holy Bandits write: "There are times when we feel the Lord might just have forgotten about us. We can't understand why certain things have happened in our lives. We want to pray but don't know what to say. Sometimes we're really angry at God, at other times we know he is right there for us. Regardless of our feelings, we thank God for being with us always, even when we think he's not.

"It is time to say goodbye to all our sorrows.... Tomorrow is our chance to look at things with new eyes, new perspective, insight. Just close your eyes and lay your head to rest on the pillow. We think about all the good things that happened today. We thank God for giving us another day. Then, we pray about the new day to come and how great life can be.

"Ready now! Take a deep breath and say to yourself, 'The day is over.' Let go of everything. Tomorrow is a new day. You can face whatever it is you need to face. Peace be with you!"

Mother of God...

Doing spiritual direction can be very inspiring, of course, but sometimes, it can be a source of deep pain for me. I am unlike any other kind of helper, because I do not believe it is my own skill or professional expertise that makes things right with the person I'm directing. Rather, the whole situation is in God's hands, and all I can do sometimes is sit, wait, and wonder. I can feel very helpless, especially when I'm called to be with someone facing death. We are all so helpless against death, aren't we? Whether it comes like a thief in the night, as with people I've seen whose loved ones have been killed in accidents or who have died swiftly and suddenly from unsuspected illnesses, or whether we have plenty of notice – an aged parent slowly wasting away, a chronic condition like cancer or AIDS asserting itself fully at last—what can we do against death?

I sit in mourning with my directees. I let the silence grow and deepen, if that's what it takes to move us toward detachment, peace, acceptance. I call upon the Spirit for wisdom. But then, afterward, alone, I take up my little rosary that I keep in my drawer and before the little icon of Mary, I light a candle and I pray the Sorrowful Mysteries, grateful in a way I'm sure many people cannot understand that there is so much room in my Catholic faith for grief and pain. The focus on suffering can be overdone, and in some ways it was in my past, but now, as I hold a sacred space open for those who come to me for direction at times of loss and grief, the Sorrowful Mysteries of the rosary are a quiet way to behold the inevitable with an open, loving heart. In this, as in so many other ways, Mary is a model.

pray for us sinners now . . .

As a child I was very devout. I remember having a great devotion to the Blessed Virgin, since I was born on the first of May, the month dedicated to the Blessed Virgin. My name was supposed to be Catherine after my grandmother, but because I was born the first day of May I was named after the Blessed Virgin. She was the mother of God and my spiritual mother, my mother too. I felt embraced and loved.

Part of my devotion to being a Catholic was saying the rosary. I would say the rosary daily, if not more often. When saying the rosary as a child, I was especially touched by, "Holy Mary, pray for us sinners now and at the hour of our death." I wanted her so much to be with me at the hour of my death. I wanted to feel the love that I experienced from her at that moment, at the moment of my death. Over and over, I said the rosary, fervently experiencing that love and the desire to go in love, with Mary by my side, to my God. From this devotion also came my desire to be pure as the Blessed Virgin was, never to sin in that way, and so I trained myself never to let a sexual thought in my head. I really wanted to be as much like her as I could be in this life.

So it is hard to think of how it was and how over the years I have changed. I have lost all of that love and devotion, and instead, I feel there's a wall between the Blessed Virgin and myself. Having only recently returned to the Catholic Church after being away for almost twenty-five years, I am still coming back slowly, and this, I do feel, is a grace which has been given to me, to be brought back and find my way home. The love I experience for my God is strong and flowing, and how blessed I feel at times! Yet, honestly, a lot of the old stuff is still there, and it does torment me.

I still have walls that I can't go through yet, and the Blessed Virgin and the rosary is one of them. When I look at the statue of the Blessed Virgin (and some other statues, too), I want to look the other way and have no part of it. I can tell you stories of what I think may have happened but I'm not sure it matters.

There was a lot of pain in my life growing up, and maybe that was what made my devotion so strong. Faith was a place to put the pain. But one particular experience with the rosary I will never forget, and maybe in retrospect it was a turning point in my devotion. I had just turned fifteen. I had three older brothers, one of which was a true brother to me. His name was Peter. He genuinely *saw* me. I felt his love and his presence with me in my life. He intervened for me in family situations, and he was my hero, my shining star.

One night I had a dream, and in the dream it felt as if someone close to me was going to die, and I could give my life in their place, but I couldn't do it. A day or two later, on Saturday morning, the day before Mother's Day and my birthday, I was on my way out to morning Mass when on the kitchen table, I saw a note saying my brother had been in a car accident, and my parents were going to New Hampshire to be with him.

I went to Mass and on the way home, my friend Katy was sitting on the stairs and told me to come into the house. My parents asked Katy's mother to tell me my brother had died. The next day, in my own house, I looked out my window to see them carrying the casket up the stairs.

As part of tradition, the rosary was said at the wake, but I can remember hating it, and I was especially furious they were saying the Glorious Mysteries. How could this be glorious! After the rosary, I wouldn't go up to the coffin, so my cousin took me in what was almost an arm lock and got someone else to do the same on the other side, and both of them were forcing me up to the coffin. Thank God for Katy's mother. She said, "Mary, do you want to go up to my house?" When I said yes, they let me go.

After my brother died, his name was never mentioned in the house again, ever. But my mother and father went to his grave every day for over a year, and forced me to go any time we all went out in the car, which was often. I had no escape, and I hated it. Once again, Katy's mother told them to stop it, and they listened to her. She had lost her husband a few months before my brother's death, and had been left with nine children to raise on her own. She told them they had to move on, and they finally stopped making me go to his grave. Three years passed before I cried for him. When I saw his fellow classmates at a memorial Mass for him and he wasn't there, then it hit me then, and I couldn't stop the tears.

My brother's death, and the rosary I clearly identify as part of his death, really put a wall up between me and God, me and Mary, me and the Church. Life has its ways, of course, and there were many other factors contributing to this wall, but Peter's death was an important part of it.

Since I have returned to church, one night I went along with some seminarians to our state prison where an inmate was going be executed, and in front of the gate, we all gathered in a circle and said the rosary together. I was surprised that I didn't feel antagonistic. Actually, instead, it felt peaceful. Another time I knew the brothers were saying the rosary in the chapel, and so I stayed away, but my timing was off and when I walked in, I got the end of it. Again I was taken back by how peaceful it was.

In one way I want to say the rosary. I want to go back to that innocence and trust I once had, but realistically I can't. I have tasted too much of life and that childlike innocence is gone. I wish I could, but the wall is there, and for now, I don't know how to get past it.

and at the hour of our death.

The sun has set over the ocean and in this desolate, windswept place of retreat, the stars are magnificent. Near the edge of the horizon, one shines very, very brightly — Venus, the evening star. Even in the light of day, it shines faintly, but now that night has come, I sit with my beads and watch it sink slowly into the depth of the sea. I would end my contemplation of these mysteries with the traditional prayers, perhaps even the long, mellifluous litany, but tonight what comes to me is a verse of a Neapolitan song, and I hear it in my grandfather's voice, low and comforting.

> When twilight's falling and the sun is setting,
> A kind of sorrow descends upon my soul.
> Beneath the window of my beloved, I'd stay forever
> But twilight's falling and the sun is setting.

I run the beads through my palm and prepare to continue from the beginning again, but first I am moved to sit quite still, mesmerized by the infinitesimally slow descent of this evening star as it continues downward, touching the ocean now so black and indistinguishable from the sky. With a small, feeble wink, it disappears, and all that is left is my memory of it, a poignant memory of what this tiny bright spot at the edge of the world once looked like when I had the good fortune to see it high above the horizon in all its glory.

Amen.

The Glorious
Mysteries

First Glorious Mystery

Resurrection

So they drew near to the village to which they were going. He appeared to be going further, but they constrained him, saying, "Stay with us, for it is toward evening and the day is now far spent." So he went in to stay with them. When he was at table with them, he took the bread and blessed and broke it, and gave it to them. And their eyes were opened and they recognized him, and he vanished out of their sight. They said to each other, "Did not out hearts burn within us while he talked to us on the road, while he opened to us the scriptures?"

(Luke 24:28–32)

Hail, Mary...

Anticipating a long and intense experience at the opera in the afternoon that Sunday, I decided last night to do body and soul a kindness and go to Newman Hall up the street for Sunday Mass. Skipping my usual 10 a.m. attendance at my own parish in San Francisco is something I rarely do, since I love Most Holy Redeemer and always leave feeling inspired and energized. But today, given the intense religiosity of the opera I am going to be seeing—*St. François d'Assise* by Olivier Messaien—going to my regular Mass would make for a long day. Instead, I just nip up the street to Newman Hall in Berkeley.

Because daily Mass at Newman is usually a quiet, prayerful experience, I imagine that 7:30 a.m. on Sunday is likewise, and the relatively empty parking lot confirms my suspicion. The space there, a big, 1960s style modernist sanctuary, has grown on me over the years, and the very aspects of it that people dislike – gray, cold, high, wide, big, a place where the people get lost – are the very aspects that I have come to appreciate. Its breadth is a form of open-arm welcome, its height a spaciousness that draws the eye and spirit upward. The unprepossessing color of the walls removes all distraction, and even its occasional chilliness is an invitation for us to warm it up with our own inner fire. In this place I can be alone with my God and in community with his people.

Then there's the crucifix...

All the sanctuary appointments – altar, lectern, tabernacle, seats, and crucifix – were commissioned for this space from sculptor Stephen de Staebler in the 1970s, and they are unusual, perhaps even controversial works of art. Massive pieces of ceramic casting, unexpectedly organic-looking with their variable brown-gray tones and rough, unfinished surfaces, they do what great art usually does: offer a new vision of reality and elicit thereby similarly fresh and strong reactions. The tabernacle looks like a hastily excavated tomb, a niche tumbling out of the wall, dark bronze and earthy, where someone might bury a treasure or plant an urn of ashes. The gigantic naturalistic arrangements of branches and flowers that usually stand close by to it complete this impression, and the whole effect is about as far away as you can get from a tidy little gilt box flanked with two florist-shop arrangements. The altar likewise: a massive sloping mastaba rising up like a platform for sacrifice, two holes the size of oil drums drilled through it front to back. These face the congregation like a pair of blank, unseeing eyes, or, as I prefer to think of them, like twin springs from which water trickles as if from a secret underground source.

The crucifix therefore, done in this style, is nothing short of arresting. High above us all on the dimly lit, dove-gray wall hangs what looks like a dead body with emaciated limbs and hips, ash-white and limp, head shorn bald. "Concentration camp survivor" is the first thought I had when I saw him, and I know I am not alone in this association. But then, taking into account the fact that the cross upon which he lays is smooth, low and flat, my second thought was "body on a coroner's table." In either case, the effect is shocking, and as at the scene of an accident or a crime, you cannot help but continue to look at this body pinned high on its sandy-brown platform. You are irresistibly drawn to examine the folds of skin beneath the chin, peer at his eyes which sometimes seem open, sometimes closed, notice the vulnerability of the armpits and knees, feel moved by the casual, open-armed gesture being made here in death.

Then the contradictions begin to sink in, and we realize that we are not really seeing what we think we are seeing. His table-like cross is not flat against the wall but rather rests on what appears to be a carefully arranged mound of earth. The cross is lifted up by it, and very subtly it moves toward us, appearing to be slowly rising from the mound of earth supporting it even as we look. And though we are literally looking at him from below, the crucifix being mounted midway between floor and ceiling in the sanctuary, vertical and high, it dawns upon us that the relaxed flesh of his torso and face indicates instead that he is not vertical at all. Rather, he lays horizontally, as if on a bed, and it is we who are high above him, looking down from a wholly different perspective. Careful observation confirms this for us, as we notice that the cross here is neither wood nor metal nor, it seems, even ceramic, but instead, it is something soft. See, it sinks beneath his weight here and there, and, moreover, those wounds are merely indentations. They might even be shadows. If he has been pierced, he has healed or is on the way to healing. As we gaze upward then, we simultaneously gaze downward, and from that position, he no longer looks like a corpse. For all his pallor, easily attributed to his asceticism, after all, we may have been completely mistaken. He might well just be asleep, sprawled wide and comfortable, as some people do when alone in bed, arms open, face peaceful, resting on the earth behind him.

But once more, this time dramatically, the perspective shifts again. As we continue to look, we see how the raised mound beneath the surface where he lies resembles a three-dimensional geographical map of the earth's surface, the cracks in the ceramic appearing to be rivers, the inclines of the ridges representing mountains and hills, and this perception changes the scale of everything for the viewer. This body which seemed so close, which we thought we were examining from a place of such uncomfortable, even clinical intimacy, appears positively enormous, cosmic, all-encompassing. If the background of this cross is the earth, then we are being given here a view of Christ as if from outer space. He hovers above the whole globe, his peaceful arms flung open wide across land, sea, and river.

For a whole semester of Christology in seminary, we tortured tradition with unrelenting questions, hoping our persistence would lead church fathers and modern theologians to at last give up the mystery and make it all plain to us, turning the questions and the answers this way and that way, wanting to know what the women who loved him wanted to know that day when they first laid eyes on the empty tomb. How can a man be both dead and alive? How does Christ come to me personally, intimately, and at the same time be known by the whole universe as Lord of all? How is it possible that Jesus is both fully divine and fully human?

The crucifix at Newman in a single stroke provides a convincing answer to how the paradoxes of Christ's nature can, each one of them, express a truth without contradiction, and it does so in that ingenious way given only to the arts. Paradox is a matter of perspective, says this crucifix to us all. Just approach him here with your own mortal senses, and see how it is possible to see Christ from above and below, to feel him near and distant, both particular and universal, to perceive him dead and know him to be alive. Here the opposites come together, here in this crucified, rising, glorified Son of God.

I have never been here on Sunday so early before, and so I am a bit disturbed to see, after getting settled in the pew, that someone must have been cleaning the lights last night, for a little circle of a spotlight is misdirected at the cross, falling not the way it usually should, softly illuminating the whole of the corpus, but rather obliquely aimed across his thighs and loincloth. That's a shame, I think to myself. I dearly love this crucifix and have had many conversations with my Lord before it. You'd think someone would have noticed and fixed it before Sunday masses begin.

But once again, the genius of the creator shows itself to me, catches me short, me in my limited vision, my aesthetic self-assurance. On my way up to communion, I look up again almost automatically, fixing my eyes upon his image behind the priest as I prepare to receive his body and drink the fruit of his life, and I realize then that I was wrong. What shines on the cross this morning is not a spotlight. It is the sun, angled through the back window, a pale but brilliant circle of autumn that now rests on his chest, moving slowly upward and across, his face still in shadow before us but his heart bright with day.

full of grace . . .

In late September, I went to Europe with my brother to visit our grandfather's home in Holic, Slovakia. We grew up next door to my Slovak grandfather and grandmother, and my intention when planning this trip was to stay at the Pistany Spa, a mineral hot springs that my grandfather visited on many of his trips. Anyway, before leaving, I met up with a parishioner friend of mine who had recently visited Medjugorje, and during our time together, I told him my HIV-positive status. He shared with me some of his experiences at Medjugorje, encouraging me to consider making a visit if there was anyway possible. I said that I would try; my schedule was very full but I might be able to squeeze it in at the end.

The whole trip seemed to be going according to plan once we were over there. We happened to make the acquaintance of a woman at the spa who told us about her life and her troubled marriage. She, too, like my friend in the parish, had visited Medjugorje to sort things out. During our conversation, she told us that while she was in Medjugorje, her rosary turned gold. When I heard this, I turned to my brother and said that I would pass out if my rosary turned gold.

Later on, as my brother and I were preparing to leave for Milan, who comes running up to our car but this woman, to say goodbye — or so I think. As we made our departure, she handed me an envelope containing a two-page letter along with a violet colored rosary on a silver chain. Along with the names of various people to see, a place to stay, and events that I should participate in when I visit Medjugorje, she ended her letter to me by writing, "You're a lucky one. Our Lady herself has invited you. Just be a guest of Our Lady. Don't go looking for miracles or visions, the biggest miracle will happen inside of you. The rosary comes from Medjugorje and was blessed there. I have prayed on this rosary and it wants to accompany you on your trip."

Once again, all seemed to go according to plan. My brother and I parted company in Milan, where he set out for a Paris trade show, and I headed for Venice. And yet as I was driving on the freeway in the north of Italy, I noticed the envelope containing both the letter and the rosary. Fumbling with the envelope, I took out the rosary and began to pray. And as I prayed and drove, I began to weep – not gentle crying but a deep sobs of sorrow and anguish. I decided then to bypass Venice and drive directly into Yugoslavia, to Medjugorje. I was on an adventure, a spiritual one at that.

When I arrived in town, I followed the instructions in the letter given to me by my chance acquaintance. I planned to stay only three days and two nights. As directed, I immediately went to the home of one of the older residents in Medjugorje. He spoke German, and with the help of an interpreter, I managed to convey to him that I needed a room for only two nights. As it turned out, the whole bottom suite of rooms were open for only two nights. He expected an entire group of German pilgrims for the third night. Not giving it a second thought, I took his invitation to stay.

After this unlikely series of circumstances, I immediately went to my room, reread the letter, and noted that it was suggested that I write a letter to Our Lady. I knelt down first to pray and as I prayed I wrote, not only for myself, but also for all of my friends, my clients that had died of AIDS, for deceased family members. I wept again for about an hour, and when I finished the letter, I planned to give it to one of the Medjugorje visionaries, Viska, who was said to have the power and grace of healing.

I arrived at Viska's home where she was speaking to a group of Italian pilgrims under a grape arbor. As I approached the group, she stopped her talk as if she had been waiting for me. Not understanding a word, I listened and when she finished her talk, I made eye contact with her, smiled, and handed her my letter. I took off running so as not to miss Father Jozo, the parish priest that protected the visionary children when the visions first started.

Father Jozo walked out from the sacristy and spoke for what seemed a short time. His melodic voice was periodically interrupted with church bells. At times, I would look at the light filtering through the stained glass windows and felt that grace had somehow filtered back into my life. Fr. Jozo spoke for over an hour about the apparitions, and at the end of his talk, I noticed Fr. Jozo blessing people lined up at the altar railing. I thought that since I was here, I might as well get a blessing from this priest, who seemed to be a truly holy man. I was nearly the last in line, near the door for a quick getaway, when Fr. Jozo came up to me. He began to pray, laying his hands first on my head, then over my heart, then touching my back, and eventually over my heart once again and in the end, finally, my head. I suddenly felt lightheaded, heard a voice in English say, "Don't be afraid,"and I felt Fr. Jozo touch my forehead with the palm of his hand and say "Anima." At that moment, I fell back. I felt as though an electric impulse passed through my body. I lay on the church floor and could not move or speak.

the Lord is with you.

After what seemed like several minutes, I regained my senses and ran out of the church, totally disoriented. I wandered until I found the bus going back to where I was staying, all the time wondering about the power of this place and what was happening here. At dinner, I again met a minister from West Berlin, and he explained to me what it meant to be "slain in the Spirit," which was what I had experienced. I had never heard of such a thing. As he put it, the Holy Spirit had touched me, and this touch is a pure and powerful spiritual gift. At the end of dinner, the minister asked if I would like to accompany him to an Adoration of the Blessed Sacrament, a devotion I hadn't attended in at least fifteen years, so I agreed, not knowing what to expect.

When we arrived at the church, the church was packed, but the minister took me right to the front. We knelt on the marble floor in front of the pews and in front of the main altar, as the service began. The only word I have to describe this experience is that it was sublime — the congregation singing in five languages, a rosary recited, and the pastor praying in English, Croatian, Italian, French, and Aramaic. By the end of the service, I was ready to go back to my room and sleep, emotionally and physically exhausted by the events of the day. However, the minister insisted that I go to Apparition Hill and say goodbye to Our Lady.

Now I thought that this was strange, but he insisted and lent me his flashlight to use. Having made my way to the top of the hill, I lit a candle and I began to pray the fifteen decades of the rosary. Once again, time ceased to exist. I was no longer cold, nor did I feel the rocks as I knelt near the cross marking an apparition site. After I finished the rosary, I followed the path down to the bottom again, when I heard someone ringing a dinner bell, but as I approached the area where the bell sounded, there was no one there. I panicked. Here I was, alone, in a place that I did not know and I was sure that I had begun to have auditory hallucinations. I ran back to the town of Medjugorje, where I stopped at a bar and had a beer to calm my nerves.

I needed to reflect on all that had happened in this two-day visit. Was I making all this up? Or was God revealing himself to me through the Blessed Mother? Were these delusions? Or was my soul finally opening to the real power of the Spirit? Would I, too, be healed, as many had been here? And how in the world would I know if all these happenings were of divine origin or simply my own craziness? With all these thoughts and questions buzzing around, I finished my beer and walked back to my room.

As I undressed for bed, I reached into my pocket and pulled out the silver rosary that had been given to me, only to stop and stare in amazement. There in my hand, the chain which had been a bright silver was now gold, deep, gleaming, unmistakably gold. How…? Why…? Suddenly I started to weep, and spontaneously thanked Our Lady for the sign that I needed. All that had happened to me was not my imagination. God was here, with me, in this place, and the proof was right here in my hand.

Blessed are you among women…

Something just clicked. I suddenly felt the power of the mysteries and the rosary. Rather than seeing the mysteries simply as a kind of review of Jesus' life for those who didn't know his story, I realized one day that the mysteries were not about reviewing facts, but about feeling what happened. The mysteries are a glimpse through Mary's eyes, into living what happened to Jesus as Mary saw and lived it.

By praying Mary's rosary, I see how something so beautiful and precious as human life can be taken away and brutally killed, but to truly walk in the spirit of Mary means also experiencing all her feelings, including rebirth, forgiveness, and closure. To crucify Jesus all over again doesn't take anything more than mistreating or mocking a fellow coworker or classmate, and all these little violences need to be changed by coming around to Mary's way of thinking, seeing, and being. She took her dead son off the cross, but she didn't attack or kill the guards. She wanted justice, but she forgave. If we are to put an end to the killing of innocent people on our own soil and around the world, we must be open, as Mary was, to a rebirth in our thinking, a forgiveness in our spirit, and a closure on our violence.

and blessed is the fruit of your womb, Jesus.

When you asked me about the rosary, I initially felt as if that topic had no "juice" for me. As I reflected on it, I could see, well, that's not really true. At one point in my life, the rosary carried a lot of juice—when I was in the Army and sure I was bound for the priesthood

At seventeen, in November of my first year in college, I lost my mother to cancer. For that rest of the year, I lost all interest in my studies, which led to my thinking that I should go into the military, that it would provide me an opportunity to sort out my thoughts and feelings. After basic training and duty in Washington, D.C., I was sent to Japan, and being at the time a very inexperienced, grieving eighteen-year-old based in Tokyo, I soon lost my virginity to a young woman who hung around bars in order to meet GIs. It was an experience without passion, love, lust, or even drunkenness, which left me "blah." As a result, I became a rather isolated lost soul, ever more certain my true passion belonged solely in service as a priest for the Lord.

Shortly after this pivotal event, I met the dean of the international school of Sophia University in Tokyo, a Jesuit Father who taught the rudimentary courses in philosophy. He took me under his wing for the rest of my stay in the suburbs. He suggested wisely that I defer the priesthood decision until I had completed undergraduate studies and encouraged me to develop a more regular prayer life. Thus in the army, I joined several other young military men reciting the rosary four afternoons a week in a small chapel reserved for the Blessed Sacrament right on our compound, with the local chaplain, and sometimes, this elderly Jesuit mentor of mine.

Fifty years later, I can still see myself there now in prayer, and it strikes me that my experience with the rosary then is the same mental state I have since experienced with Hindu *mala* beads and later with Buddhist beads. All are ritual ways into a state of conscious nonattachment, the intoned repetition of prayers keeping the ego-mind out of "thought" and immersed in feeling. But there is more to the rosary, I see now, for my prayer then was also the veneration of Mary, the person I began to feel, in a very human way, as "my" mother, understanding even in my own undeveloped soul her compassion in the three types of mysteries she experienced

Looking back in imagination at my state of mind as a boy away from home, a Catholic altar boy who had further alienated himself by "sinning" in this distant land, it is not hard, as the clinical psychologist I have now become, to see in my prayer of the rosary the safekeeping into which I placed my own mother, too soon taken from my younger brother and I at a time when we needed her most. Add to this, a culture that did not accept male grief, which told us to stand up as men and not to cry: only decades later in the study of psychology did I begin to work through this grief over the loss of my mother. Then and only then, so many years later, was I able to take my mother out of the distant heaven in which I had placed her and use the pain of missing her to free myself, to take up my own cross and more fully live the life I was meant to live, rather than the life of "good son."

This is how I understand the phrase about Mary from the Gospel, "she held all these things within her heart." Setting up

Mary as my mother saved my fragile self, closeted the human memory of my mother, letting me see only a suffering saint, a "victim" of my father, her husband. With time, I have grown far beyond that poor lost, late adolescent to become a man capable of affirming the feminine, working hard to hold in myself a balance between male and female energies. I must admit that prior to this change in me, I was a righteous, defended, independent man. Looking back on this providential encounter with Mary through the rosary, I'm glad I listened to the chaplain. I suspect I'd have been a tormented priest instead of a happy grandfather, for my true priesthood is to be the compassionate psychologist I am now. And in all of this Mary and the rosary played a part.

Holy Mary

I called my little rosary business Laetare Designs because "laetare" is Latin for "rejoice," and the rosaries I make are acts of rejoicing. I rejoice in the beauty of the materials given to me, the wonder of God's creation held in my hands thankfully and thoughtfully. I rejoice in the gift of the rosary as a prayerful practice, a daily time of peace, comfort, and grace through my devotion to Mary and her son, our Savior, Jesus Christ. And I rejoice in my capacity to share the rosaries I make with those who will take these beads and make them a part of their own devotions, in times of trouble and of joy.

Variations on the rosary are infinite, limited only by inspiration and the materials at hand. Among the many excellent and devoted rosary-makers I have met, each of us has been called to this work in his or her own way and time. All our work has its own style, just as we all approach God in our own way and language.

For me, I am drawn to the chance encounter, the found object, forgotten parts, and neglected beads. I comb bead outlets for closeouts and castoffs, odd lots of gemstones, quality glass beads in discontinued colors and shapes. I wander through estate sales, auctions, and flea markets, on the look-out for old rosaries, often broken and discarded, with unusual vintage centers or lovely crucifixes with a bit of tarnish, easily removed. Many a peculiar necklace, given to me by a friend, reveals its true, sacred beauty when restrung with care. Likewise, many an old bead, medal and cross upon which countless prayers were said, has been given new and restored homes. New beads and contemporary parts have their place, of course, but it was the stone which was despised and rejected that became the foundation of the church, was it not? My faith is a resurrection faith, so it is especially gratifying to me to give old parts new life, to honor the risen Christ in a rosary that mirrors his own dying and rising.

Mother of God . . .

Christopher Bamford writes: "In other words, the resurrection is a perpetual, continuous event. 'The great life,' in Joa Bolendas's phrase, is always present. This is one meaning of the Christian mystery — that as Christ is always being crucified in all suffering and pain, so that whenever we suffer or witness suffering that suffering is part of Christ's passion, so too he is always rising, and the resurrection is always there for us, whether we are aware of it or not. The deaths we die — the falls, the betrayals, the separations, the losses — are important but equally important are our risings, our experiences of new life flooding in. In a garden, though spring comes but once a year, in another sense it is always spring. There is always the greenness in the sap: metamorphosis, death, and resurrection are continuous....

"Saying the rosary, entering the healing field of the garden, we live in two currents of time flowing simultaneously. The great life, the future, the resurrection flow into the small life of dying, becoming open, letting go, these two currents crossing at every moment, in every image, so that they become one. In traditional terms, this is the marriage or union of Christ with Mary. Living at the juncture, we are healed — for a moment.... We are always dying and rising again, and if we can let go of our linear, spatial scenarios and enter into the living sacred time of the garden, that holy rain of grace will water and heal us."

pray for us sinners now...

John Paul II writes: "In Christ, God has truly assumed a 'heart of flesh.' Not only does God have a divine heart, rich in mercy and in forgiveness, but also a human heart, capable of all the stirrings of affection. If we needed evidence for this from the Gospel, we could easily find it in the touching dialogue between Christ and Peter after the Resurrection: 'Simon, son of John, do you love me?' Three times this question is put to Peter, and three times he gives the reply: 'Lord, you know that I love you' (John 21:15–17). Over and above the specific meaning of this passage, so important for Peter's mission, none can fail to recognize the beauty of this triple repetition, in which the insistent request and the corresponding reply are expressed in terms familiar from the universal experience of human love. To understand the rosary, one has to enter into the psychological dynamic proper to love.

"One thing is clear: although the repeated *Hail, Mary* is addressed directly to Mary, it is to Jesus that the act of love is ultimately directed, with her and through her. The repetition is nourished by the desire to be conformed ever more completely to Christ, the true programme of the Christian life. St. Paul expressed this project with words of fire: 'For me to live is Christ and to die is gain' (Phil. 1:21). And again: 'It is no longer I that live, but Christ lives in me' (Gal. 2:20). The rosary helps us to be conformed ever more closely to Christ until we attain true holiness."

and at the hour of our death.

This connection to the rosary with God's living creation reveals itself in the way I was taught to dispose of old rosary beads. Because of my interest in creating rosaries that have a style both contemporary and traditional, I found that second-hand stores, antique shops, and online auction sites are very likely to have old rosaries with very beautiful old parts, some of which may date back to the early 1900s and are fairly easily restored with a bit of elbow grease and polish. Once I took apart the rosary for the center and crucifix, I really didn't know how to deal properly with leftover damaged and unusable beads. I couldn't in good conscience just throw them into the trash, not after thinking about how years' and years' worth of prayers had been said on them or how a certain nun or brother might have worn this rosary as part of their habit for fifty or sixty years. And yet, my bag of unusable old beads and chains was growing. When all else fails, ask someone older and wiser—a good rosary-maker rule.

The answer came back from my friend Margot via e-mail: bury the beads or burn them. The idea that the traditional way to dispose of rosary beads was precisely the way one might dispose of a human body was a rather inescapable observation, at the same chilling and comforting. It certainly felt right. But

I haven't quite gotten around to finding a place in my garden
or my fireplace for all those old, chipped coco beads and tar-
nished chains. Perhaps sometime in the month of devotion to
the Holy Rosary, I'll make a pilgrimage up to the hills and put
the whole lot beneath a beautiful oak or perhaps a little willow
sapling down by the waterfront.

Amen.

Ascension

"It is not for you to know the times or season which the Father has fixed by his own authority. But you shall receive power when the Holy Spirit has come upon you, and you shall be my witnesses in Jerusalem and in all Judea and Samaria and to the end of the earth." And when he had said this, as they were looking on, he was lifted up, and a cloud took him out of their sight. And while they were gazing into heaven as he went, behold, two men stood by them in white robes and said, "Men of Galilee, why do you stand looking into heaven? This Jesus, who was taken up from you into heaven, will come in the same way you saw him go into heaven." (Acts 1:7–11)

Hail, Mary...

A circle made of loving arms. A garden of fragrant prayer. An unavoidable noose. An enclosure of safety. The rosary can be all these things, depending on what eyes you have. How you image the rosary says much about your personal experience of the Lord.

For me, I see the rosary as a doorway or a window onto transcendence, and in particular, bodily transcendence. Indeed, of all the mysteries, the glorious mysteries are the most explicitly Christian, in that they are all about the physical transformation that is possible for each us through Christ. His path is not a spiritualizing, mental, philosophical change of life but a complete reordering of the physical universe. The dead are raised. Bodies ascend into heaven, are redeemed from corruption and decay. The Holy Spirit of God pervades the world of matter and changes how we speak, how we hear, how we move. Out of this unconditional embrace of the physical world as God's creation, which is the foundation of Jesus' very Jewish faith, he lived out his earthly life—joining his divinity to our humanity—to show the possible transformation of that universe—so that we might join in his divinity.

Mary precedes the rest of us in her utter willingness to let her physical life be transformed by this Spirit, by this Christ within her, and her prayer of the rosary opens for us the same portal into a different life. Dare we step through it into full belief in the power of such literal physical transformation? Dare we hold the risen Christ's hand, as she did, and let our mortal selves be made whole, glorious, perfect? Can we let ourselves ascend, go beyond the limits of senses, the confines of our doubts, to perceive how we participate even now in the eternal life of God, not in spite of our bodies, because precisely through our very embodiment as the crown of creation?

Jesus does not cast off his mortal body in the Ascension. It is not merely his spirit or soul that floats up to the clouds, like some cartoon ghost or a wisp of smoke. Rather, his risen and glorified body, whole and entire, goes home, the body that ate and drank, that laid hands upon the sick, that let itself be pierced and hung. The ascension of Christ is the clearest affirmation in all of our tradition that we are, as physical beings, indeed "fearfully and wonderfully made." Our bodies are not so much detritus to be sloughed off or neglected. They are rather the very vehicle of our transcendence.

The open door of the rosary invites us to step through these glorious mysteries, to ascend with Christ into the heavens and to imagine ourselves, soul and body, transformed and glorified, redeemed and raised.

full of grace . . .

When I began to pray the rosary again as an adult, after being given a set of hematite beads strung on fishing line by a missionary friend from Central America, I hadn't prayed the rosary in a very long time, and for some reason, I had gotten it in my head that the third glorious mystery was the Transfiguration. So there I was, for the good part of a year, meditating faithfully on the "wrong" mystery. Somehow the fact that the Transfiguration was out of chronological order didn't trouble me, I think, because I always especially loved that episode of Christ's life, and there are many things about it that I find glorious. Its explicit reference to Jesus' Jewishness was very welcome to me. His appearing there on the mountaintop with Moses and Elijah, the two great holy men of his tradition, reminds us unmistakably of his Judaism, too easily and too disastrously forgotten by Christians. The scene also reminds us that he tried, as did both Moses and Elijah, to call his own people to reform their spirituality and religious practice, and he met with similar hard-heartedness and opposition. Jesus was a prophet from a long line of powerful prophets, so, we, too, are meant to be prophets as his followers, critics of our own tradition when it deviates from the law of love for God and neighbor. And like Elijah, Jesus rose into heaven and is expected to come again sometime, perhaps even show up to take his place at our next Seder meal. His prophetic presence endures as a past reality and an ever-present future potentiality. We forget the radical, prophetic Judaism of Jesus at our peril, and my meditations upon the Transfiguration in place of the Ascension mystery now appears to me to be a kind of *felix culpa,* a fortuitous spiritual slip-of-the-mind.

I was eventually, quite humbly, corrected by a child's "How to Pray the Rosary" booklet left behind one Sunday in the pew. After a bit of embarrassment, I began to contemplate the proper mystery from then on, like a good Catholic boy, deciding on my own that probably no act of contrition was needed. An honest mistake.

But a meaningful one, I believe, especially now that contemplation of the mystery of the Transfiguration has been included among the new set of mysteries recommended last year by Pope John Paul II. The Transfiguration most certainly prefigures the Ascension, just as the miracle at Cana prefigures the institution of the Eucharist, and as its prefiguration — and my own lapse — indicate, one of the essential meanings of the Ascension of Christ can be found in his call as prophet.

Thus I have ended up more or less meditating upon the same questions as I pray the rosary's second glorious mystery: how am I called to be prophetic, in my church, in the secular world, in my relationships and work? How is God trying to speak through me? What higher wisdom am I meant to convey or to display? And when I encounter opposition, ridicule, persecution, dismissal, and contempt for my prophetic stance, am I willing to choose to do God's will as Jesus did and speak out at whatever personal price?

the Lord is with you.

One of my favorite places to pray the rosary is on a plane, not just to calm my anxiety about flying, but is there any better place to contemplate the glorious mysteries than from the middle of the sky? I have had some truly glorious meditations up there —

the cabin dark and still after food service, the hum of the engines making everyone sleepy, my airline blanket arranged on my lap to conceal my discreetly held beads so I don't "display my piety before others." I keep my little window shade pushed up just enough next to me to give me a vision of the clear blue sky above a vast floor of clouds below so white they look almost black in the sunlight. Here and there the clouds part to reveal the enormous variety of the earth below: patchwork fields, snaking roads and rivers, sometimes nothing but a silver sheet of ocean, shimmering royal blue-green. Up here I let my spirit join with the ascending Christ, merge my consciousness with his serene and loving detachment, looking down at it all and praying that I might remember how silent, how beautiful it is from this distance. What a miracle that we get such a God's-eye view, and not just in our imagination! So this is what it is like to ascend, to see it all, to love it all.

Blessed are you among women . . .

I'm fortunate enough to be able to work at home, thanks to the wonders of modern technology, but the downside is that it can get kind of claustrophobic and isolating. So what I do between phone calls and faxes a lot of times is what I humorously call "getting high," which isn't what you might think. What I mean by "getting high" is literally getting high: I get in my car and I head up to the top of the hills near my home where there is a beautiful look-out point at the end of a little trail. Not a lot of people know about it, so most of the time I can count on being there by myself, especially in the middle of a weekday, and it is a perfect place to practice contemplative prayer, for all I can hear is the breeze through the eucalyptuses. The view of the valley, the lakes, the cows grazing, the clouds in the sky is so inspiring, I find myself just automatically praying. I do a lot of different kinds of prayer—sometimes breath-work, sometimes nature contemplation, but I really love the rosary, especially sitting way up high there at Lookout Point.

A friend of mine gave me a Czech rosary made of dark-red and gold beads which I keep in the glove compartment of my car, and I like to say the Glorious Mysteries up there, letting my spirit rise. Mary herself is still a little bit of an enigma for me, but when I meditate on the events of her life, what I know of them in the New Testament, I am impressed by — or maybe I should say that I feel inspired to emulate her detachment, her ability to rise above it all. Right from the start she rose above herself and let the Divine Force shine through her. I don't do this very easily myself, and running my own agency, pretty much on my own for most things, it's an ability I would like to have. I don't let things go. I get all involved in "down here," when what I should be doing is "ascending" and letting myself "get high." So my prayer practice up there, especially the rosary mysteries, are a way for me to return to a higher consciousness, and even when I'm back home, I try to remember the way it looked up there when I find myself getting pushy or anxious. I don't know if wearing the beads around my neck like some women do would be a helpful reminder. Maybe it would.

and blessed is the fruit of your womb, Jesus.

The recursiveness of the rosary is a continual delight to me, as is the continual alternation between movements upward and movements downward in the images. In this sense the rosary is like a dance between heaven and earth. The descent of the spirit in the Annunciation, dwelling for a time in fleshly form, then ascends again in the Passion, first in agonized prayer and then definitively on the cross. Giving up his spirit precedes Jesus' rising again, first rising to life and then rising to heaven, beginning yet another cycle of up-and-down, as his Ascension precedes another descent of the spirit which itself precedes yet another upward movement, Mary's own Assumption. If we followed the endless circle around again, tracing infinity with our fingers on the beads, the spirit would again descend on Mary, embody itself, and over and over again the story would go. Indeed, the cyclical genius of the rosary discloses a certain truth about the life of spirit: as we ourselves cycle through the days, weeks, and months of chronological time, the Spirit comes and goes, up and down. Our task, perhaps our only task, is to take the next step and keep the infinite dance going, round and round, up and down.

Holy Mary . . .

I'm curious to see how people devoted to the rosary will react to the pope's announcement of the new "Mysteries of Light." What he is recommending here isn't really something new or even all that different. In fact, at the beginning of the rosary, the practice had no mysteries or episodes from the life of Christ connected to the prayers at all, but simply required a knotted prayer rope and 150 Our Fathers. It wasn't until much later that the meditations on the life of Christ, the *vita Christi* mysteries, were added, and even then, for quite some time, there was much variation on what episodes of his life were contemplated, varying from region to region, country to country. Indeed, the earliest known pictorial representation of the fifteen rosary mysteries, from Ulm, Germany, in 1483, shows that the Last Judgment was the final mystery for contemplation, rather than the Coronation of the Virgin.

In my personal experience, I know that the rosary has the capacity to transcend tradition and custom. I have spoken with certain Protestants who substitute the more explicitly Marian mysteries of the Joyful cycle with the so-called life mysteries, taking episodes of Christ's life like the wedding of Cana, walking on the water, the Transfiguration and so forth, and using them as a focus of meditations. While on retreats, I came up with a set of the "healing mysteries," letting my soul dwell upon the various healings performed by Christ during the course of his earthly ministry that I felt drawn to: the casting out of the Gerasene demoniac, the raising of Lazarus, the healing of the woman with a hemorrhage, the cure of the centurion's daughter, and, finally, perhaps stretching the category a little, exposing his wounded side to Thomas as a way to cure doubt and lack of faith. These episodes of Jesus bringing the marginalized and outcast into the circle of his compassion as well as attending to people he loved and counted among his intimates were especially enriching for me to contemplate, at a time of my life when I felt in need of spiritual and physical healing.

Another variation that came to me grew out of repeated experiences of Padre Pio I have had over the course of my life, such that I created a seven-decade chaplet out of petrified wood beads for my personal use. After Padre Pio's canonization in June 2002, I prayed a novena of this rosary before his September 23 feast day as a way to help me gain a more profound understanding of the seven graces or virtues that Padre Pio embodied in his life and faith: poverty, chastity, mystical prayer, the stigmata, obedience, penitence and healing.

The fifteen-decade Dominican rosary, with which most of us are familiar, is in fact only one tradition, and what the Holy Father is recommending — to use various episodes of Christ's public ministry as a focus of contemplation — is not at all unheard of and has a sound precedent in the history of the rosary itself. He has done us a favor by reminding us that the rosary can and does transcend narrow customs, and it is a good thing for people to feel permission to be creative, and even innovative, around using the beads in ways that are individually inspiring.

Mother of God . . .

When Mary is near to me, I don't hear her speak, but there is a warm presence that feels like water or honey, and sometimes I feel almost drenched in it. I had had this sensation many times during prayer earlier in my life, but I really didn't know what it was or who it was, but it is very distinct. It is the sensation you have when you know someone else is in the house but you haven't seen him or her. You feel their presence, you know somehow without really knowing. You can feel it and sense it. With Mary it is more intense, though, because it is not just an outer sensation but an inward experience as well. I can feel her with me and in me, but not Mary in and of herself. Instead it is Mary-in-Jesus. That is the only way I can say it. It isn't just her, but her love for her son and her complete oneness with his mission. I have had this experience of her presence since I was a child, and it is very uplifting for me.

pray for us sinners now . . .

Lift from my eyes, O Lord, all blindness to your beauty
Lift from my heart, O Lord, all heaviness of soul.
Lift up my mind, O Lord, to finer comprehension.
Lift up my hands, O Lord, in thanks for all made whole.

and at the hour of our death.

I love the stories after the Resurrection: Mary Magdalene searching for Jesus after the Crucifixion and finding him, only thinking that he's the gardener, or the disciples meeting a stranger on the way to Emmaus and only afterward realizing that the stranger was Jesus. This mystery always brings to mind those times in my life when a certain passage has been completed, it is like a resurrection, a new life. But ultimately, the story continues and Jesus leaves his apostles. "Where I am going, you cannot follow," because, he says to them, "unless I go, the Spirit cannot come." The Ascension reminds us how hard it can be to let go of treasured relationships, but often how necessary, how necessary to grow.

Amen.

Gift of the Spirit

*And when they had entered, they went up to the upper room
where they were staying, Peter and John and James and Andrew, Philip and Thomas, Bartholomew and Matthew, James
the son of Alphaeus and Simon the Zealot, and Judas the
son of James. All these with one accord devoted themselves
to prayer, together with the women and Mary the mother
of Jesus and with his brethren.... When the day of Pentecost
had come, they were all together in one place. And suddenly
a sound came from heaven like the rush of a mighty wind,
and it filled all the house where they were sitting. And there
appeared to them tongues as of fire, distributed and resting
on each one of them. And they were all filled with the Holy
Spirit.... (Acts 1:13–14; 2:1–4)*

Hail, Mary...

I occasionally encounter people who are unacquainted with
the essentially contemplative nature of the rosary prayer, often
Protestants of a somewhat fundamentalist or evangelical bent
who are fond of quoting Jesus' injunction not to pray as the
Gentiles do, heaping up empty phrases. What such critics of
the rosary do not understand is that I agree with them *and*
with Jesus. I do not believe that the benefit of the rosary is in
the many words we pray but instead in the opportunity those
words give us to exercise our desire to be in God's presence.

As St. Augustine so beautifully describes in his letter to Proba, this prolongation of desire is the soul of prayer and its primary spiritual benefit: "When we cherish uninterrupted desire along with the exercise of faith and hope and charity, we 'pray always.' But at certain stated hours and seasons we also use words in prayer to God, that by these signs of things we may admonish ourselves, and may acquaint ourselves with the measure of progress which we have made in this desire, and may more warmly excite ourselves to obtain an increase of its strength. For the effect following upon prayer will be excellent in proportion to the strength of the desire which precedes its utterance. What else could be intended by the words of St. Paul, when he tells us to 'pray without ceasing,' than to tell us, in so many words to 'constantly desire a happy life, which is to say eternal life, from God who alone can give it.' This life in God, therefore, is what we desire continually, and this is what we pray for without ceasing. Nevertheless, at certain hours we recall our minds from other cares and business to the business of prayer, admonishing ourselves by the words of our prayer to fix attention upon that which we desire, fanning the flame of it frequently, lest our longing for God lose its heat and become cold, or even altogether extinguished.

"Likewise, the same apostle says, 'Let your requests be made known unto God,' which is not to be understood as if by our words such requests became known to God—who after all most certainly knew of our requests before we even uttered them. Rather, we speak our requests so that they may be made known to ourselves in the presence of God. It is upon him we attend patiently with our prayers, not in the presence of other people by way of verbose and ostentatious worship....

"This is why it is neither wrong nor unprofitable for us to spend a great deal of time in prayer, as long as we do not neglect other good and necessary works to which our duty calls us, or, better still, carry out such duties as we have faithfully and thus to make of these works still yet another manner for us to 'pray without ceasing.' After all, to spend a long time in prayer is not, as some think, the same thing as to pray 'with much speaking.' Multiplied words are one thing; but a long-continued warmth of desire for God is another."

full of grace . . .

As the spirit is individually distributed to each disciple, each rosary strand has its own rhythm. The beads need to be arranged on the line of the wire in a way faithful to their own individual characteristics but also in keeping with the rosary as a whole, and I find that this is not simply a principle of good aesthetics but has a kind of deeper, symbolic spiritual meaning as well. Large beads need to be well-spaced, not too crowded. Dark beads need to be set off with accents that brighten them and bring out their color. A small delicate center shouldn't be overwhelmed by busyness and excess, and the rest of the strand should be attentive to "keep time" with each of the beads in it.

Rosaries and spiritual communities are a lot like music in this way, and as with music, it helps to have a bit of an ear and the capacity to listen. When kids are just learning to play the piano, I can hear when they've missed a beat or when the rhythm is a bit off, but some people can't pick that up. Likewise, with a rosary, I can see when the rhythm is off, if there's a little tick in the proportions, when something's irregular, or when even a lovely irregular pattern of mixed beads has become repetitious. When the rhythm of the rosary is right, no one really notices. It just looks good and feels right. But so much subtle and unspoken care has to go into making that kind of seamless, apparently effortless cooperation a reality — in a rosary or in a parish. It can be quite an art, and like an art, it takes equal parts talent, sensitivity, persistence, and God's grace.

the Lord is with you.

Before the rosary and my own rosary-making, I had never been so drawn to an inanimate item before in my life, and, believe me, I am a person who really likes "stuff." But once I tried my hand at rosary-making, it was as if I was compelled to make more, compelled to share this wonderful feeling with anyone who wanted it and compelled to make beautiful weapons against evil. And at this point, I've made over one hundred rosaries for friends and family, and I get the same reaction each time—one of pure joy and happiness. Everyone seems to fall in love with their rosaries, just as my friend told me when she gave me my first rosary and got me started. "Everyone deserves to hold a beautiful rosary while praying to our Blessed Mother," she said, and now I see she was right. That's why I make only rosaries out of beautiful beads.

I've never seen so many people become so excited over a religious object, including myself. It's the most rewarding experience. So I just keep making them. I can't stop. As long as my hands are willing, I will continue to make rosaries. This is indeed one of the most worthwhile projects I have ever been involved in.

Blessed are you among women...

My devotion to the rosary began in early childhood, and I am certain that my wonderful role model of a mother had a huge influence on me. She recently told me that she prays fourteen rosaries each day—and she is ninety-one years young, with a rosary in every coat and sweater pocket.

For me, the rosary has always been an experience of wrapping my arms around the world in prayer. Naturally, there have been times when I have been distracted while praying the rosary, especially when fatigue, stress overload, and the bombardment of external stimulation overwhelm me. But I am so grateful that our loving God and his tender Mother smile and reward our *desire* to pray, overlooking our human weakness and frailties around how we do our prayers. Even though we may not *feel* the consolation of prayer right then, love is in the will. I have learned that as long as we persevere, we are on the right track when we pray, because it is an act of love. God comes close to those who just hang in there!

Another dimension of the rosary is the way it is a window through which I can look out and see God's view of things. Often it is hard to see the whole picture when we are standing inside of the frame of a situation or a feeling. But I have discovered how frequently all these distractions seem to quiet down when I pray the rosary and when the image of embracing the whole world in my prayer captures me.

Both of these experiences of the rosary came together in a wonderful way when one of the sisters of our community visited me each day while I was recovering from back surgery in 1987. She confided that she was having great difficulty praying the rosary, as she found herself so distracted. I told her of my devotion for the rosary, how I felt as though I was wrapping my arms around the whole world when I prayed it and how doing this left me precious little time for distractions.

She liked this idea, and off she went with a dream that became a reality. She compiled a little booklet of petitions that we composed together, and together we made an audio tape of ourselves praying the rosary, incorporating these petitions with each Hail Mary. In the years since we began distributing these booklets and tapes free of charge, they have circulated into prisons, nursing homes, hospitals, and homes across the U.S., Canada, and Europe. We started with five hundred tapes at first, and we continue to distribute them with the donations we received from the tapes. Each time our supply was exhausted, we had just enough money come in through offerings to reorder another shipment to keep sending them out to the world.

In this way, our Blessed Mother is asking us to become carriers and witnesses of peace to our unpeaceful world. The rosary is such a powerful weapon for peace and reconciliation — a prayer that embraces the whole world.

and blessed is the fruit of your womb, Jesus.

Praying the rosary has made a change in my life. I hadn't prayed the rosary for quite a while and the first night I started again, it didn't really feel like a big deal, and I wasn't that into it, since it didn't feel like I was doing anything. But as I continued praying each night, I got more into it. I began to say the prayers with more meaning and started reflecting on the mysteries. That's when I entered onto a new level of prayer for me, a new closeness with God and Mary, forgetting about everything that had gone on that day — school, work, karate — just concentrating on talking to God and Mary. Through the simple rosary prayer, my life has improved a lot. I feel more content with myself and with what is going on around me, and I know that Mary is with me throughout the day, watching over me. Even if I come upon a task that seems impossible, I know that Mary will give me the strength and support to accomplish anything.

The times and events of the thirteenth century when the rosary came into being were very different from today, but today I think we have more temptations. With our good economy, we don't need to worry so much about attaining the basic

181

necessities of life. We have a lot more time and opportunity to get misdirected, to turn away from God and his ways.

Through prayer, I have come to believe that I can be an instrument of the Lord's peace in my home, in my community, and ultimately in the world. I can do this each day by how I treat everyone I personally know and each person I meet. To treat others as you would have them treat you is the rule of God, but it is not always a simple rule to carry out. The rosary helps me keep a focus on this mindset of peace and love which is God's rule for us. Right now, I'm in high school, but I believe that if I follow the rule of God over the course of my school years, when I go into the larger world, I can then be an instrument of the Lord's peace on a greater scale. With greater responsibilities, I can serve as an example and a role model, can raise my own children in the Lord's peace and in this way expand the Lord's message through them. That's the power of the rosary and Mary. Through them, anything is possible—even peace.

Holy Mary . . .

Here are just a few of the miracles of the rosary I witnessed myself in Medjugorje. The crystal rosary I bought there after a week began to reek of roses, and Medjugorje has no roses in it anywhere. They barely have enough water to irrigate their fields, so roses are out of the question. And yet, once I arrived, I began to smell roses everywhere. On the top of one of the hills there, I peeked to the left and right, thinking someone had one of those special rose-scented rosaries, but everyone was holding crystal or pearls. But when I rubbed my forehead, I realized the scent was coming from my own rosary. I handed the rosary to the young person near me, and he just gasped, the scent was so strong. The whole week we were there, the kids in the youth group loved walking behind me because they could smell the roses coming right through my backpack. When we left Medju-gorje, however, as soon as we crossed over the border into the rest of Bosnia-Herzegovina, the scent stopped from my rosary. On the other hand, one of the other ladies I was with kept notic-ing the scent of roses on her rosary until she finally gave it to someone back home.

In another mystical experience there, we were saying the rosary and during the reading of the mystery of the Annuncia-tion, we heard that the Holy Spirit breathed on Mary and that his voice was like the wind. Now, it was perfectly still and hot that day in the middle of the summer, and you could hear the locusts. But the moment the word "wind" was pronounced, a tremen-dous wind came up in the trees and bent them over almost dou-ble. It was very striking. And once again, when we got to the de-scent of the Holy Spirit, when they read that the sound of a great wind came upon them, instantly the wind came up again. In the middle of our saying the rosary, at the mention of single word, we watched being manifested what we were praying about.

The presence of the Spirit in that place was very powerful, and we were always praying quite a number of full rosaries every day in devotion, so other gifts of the Spirit came to us, too. For example, people would be praying the rosary in a foreign lan-guage we had never heard before, but we would immediately know what mystery they were on and we would just naturally begin to pray with them and follow in English. Or if someone began to sing, we would find ourselves singing in the foreign language that was being sung. It was an amazing experience, like Pentecost, I imagine.

Mother of God...

I've had many occasions to wonder whether or not my rosary-making is an art. There is no question in my mind that it is certainly a craft, not so much a craft of hands and tools but of imagination and aesthetic judgment. But an art? I've not been so sure it is — or that it isn't. The kinds of rosaries that come most naturally to me to make have very frequently solicited the comment that they are more like "art pieces" than rosaries, by which I have understood people to mean that the original designs, large size, and opulent materials of my pieces are quite different than the normal, dowdy-modest, church-store models most people see. And the possibility that my rosary-making might indeed be a form of art has led me to imagine, with some encouragement from an artist-friend of mine, to consider some day mounting an installation.

The concept already is clear to me: in a large dimly lit room, on invisible thread I would hang fifty handcrafted rosaries, each with a single soft beam of light illuminating its unique shape, as if floating in air. Each of these rosaries would be accompanied by a statement about a woman who had a decisive effect on my spiritual life, women I had personally known in this life — my grandmothers, certain friends and teachers — as well as women who are part of the community of saints: the Blessed Mother, of course, in her different manifestations, as well as women like St. Teresa of Avila, St. Catherine of Siena, and so forth. Though I haven't had the self-confidence yet to move on this idea, in part that is because I haven't yet resolved the question of whether or not the making of prayer beads is legitimately an art.

A "Letter to Artists," which Pope John Paul II wrote a few years ago, was helpful to me around this question, and to the extent that my rosary-making comes from the spiritual perceptiveness he describes here, then I am comfortable owning my rosary-making as art: "Every genuine artistic intuition goes beyond what the senses perceive and, reaching beneath reality's surface, strives to interpret its hidden mystery. The intuition itself springs from the depths of the human soul, where the desire to give meaning to one's own life is joined by the fleeting vision of beauty and of the mysterious unity of things. All artists experience the unbridgeable gap which lies between the work of their hands, however successful it may be, and the dazzling perfection of the beauty glimpsed in the ardour of the creative moment: what they manage to express in their painting, their sculpting, their creating is no more than a glimmer of the splendour which flared for a moment before the eyes of their spirit.

"Believers find nothing strange in this: they know that they have had a momentary glimpse of the abyss of light which has its original wellspring in God. Is it in any way surprising that this leaves the spirit overwhelmed as it were, so that it can only stammer in reply? Every genuine art form in its own way is a path to the inmost reality of human beings and of the world. It is therefore a wholly valid approach to the realm of faith, which gives human experience its ultimate meaning. That is why the Gospel fullness of truth was bound from the beginning to stir the interest of artists, who by their very nature are alert to every 'epiphany' of the inner beauty of things."

pray for us sinners now ...

I was taught that it was good to use the mysteries to contemplate various aspects of the nature of God as revealed in Christ or as exemplified by Mary, so for the descent of the Spirit I focus my meditations around the theme of generosity. God pours out his Spirit upon the disciples, and this is his generosity. God continues to pour our his Spirit upon us even today, and endow us each and every one of us with gifts, talents, inspiration, pleasures, wisdom and will, and this, too, is his generosity. How have I, as a teacher, used those gifts and talents in a way that inspires or instructs others today? I take some time at the end of the day with my rosary to go over how I have been generous with myself, or not. Then I take the last part of that mystery to go over in my mind the various acts of generosity of others toward me. Who yielded to me in traffic? Who did I get a card from? How has my family appreciated me? What blessings are still unfolding? I feel a little Pollyannaish around sharing this, but the glorious mysteries are meant to be glorious, aren't they? I find meditating upon the great generosity of the Lord and the gifts of the Spirit in my life an excellent antidote to many of my own spiritual and emotional ills.

and at the hour of our death.

The most recent miracle I have seen because of the rosary happened to a very dear friend of mine. She teaches catechism at my parish, and she was diagnosed with leukemia, which came upon her very quickly. First, all she had was a headache and then five days later, she was in the ICU. All her organs had started to shut down, and her condition was so serious that the priests there told her husband that in all likelihood, by next week they would be doing her funeral.

However, Our Lady told me that we were about to see a miracle and that I was just to keep praying. Practically the entire parish crowded into the hospital waiting room for intensive care, and for two weekends in a row, we prayed full rosaries for her. I also sent petitions for her cure to all the major sites, Fatima, Lourdes, Medjugorje, and had a priest here who is well known for his healing ministry to put her on his list.

After a few days and many rosaries, she just woke up, not appearing to realize that she really had been at death's door, and she asked her husband why he was looking so concerned. What is miraculous is they can't find any cancer in her any more, and, though the doctors swear it is not possible for an organ that has shut down to reanimate itself, all her organs are fine now.

At this point, she is completely well, has gotten back to her teaching, and is now going around to talk about her healing experience. The only thing she can remember from that time is that she recalls a priest coming in to speak with her, telling her that her experience was going to be like that of Lazarus, but she didn't know what he was talking about. She didn't even realize she was in a coma. During the vision, she called him "father" but he corrected her and said to her that he wasn't a priest. Now she realizes that she must have been talking to an angel, since nobody else saw him in her room.

Our Lady told me afterward that the purpose of this miracle was really for our parish, since so many of us at the time had lost sight of the fact that miracles do happen. She said to me, "God does exist, and he shows himself through miracles. This will be a wake-up call to all those in RCIA that have their doubts." And it certainly was. And now my friend has in turn started a ministry of her own, going down to intensive care to pray the rosary with whoever is there. You can't pray the rosary without having these experiences.

Amen.

Assumption

When finally the Blessed Virgin had fulfilled the course of this life, and was now to be called out of this world, all the Apostles were gathered together from each region to her house... and behold the Lord Jesus came with His angels and, receiving her soul, entrusted it to the Archangel Michael and departed. At the break of day the Apostles lifted the body with the couch and laid it in the sepulchre, and they guarded it awaiting the coming of the Lord. And behold the Lord again stood by them, and commanded that the holy body be taken up and borne on a cloud into Paradise, where now, reunited with [her] soul and rejoicing with the elect, it enjoys the good things of eternity which shall never come to an end. (St. Gregory of Tours)

Hail, Mary...

The mystery of the Assumption had for a long time eluded me in my prayers. The Lutheran household in which I was raised had very little of the mystical about its religious experience—we were very down-to-earth and matter-of-fact about our church going and community service. While part of my family was Catholic, my experience of their faith was primarily at weddings or funerals, in addition to occasional jovial visits by my second-cousin, a diocesan priest. My going to a public school meant that I had little interaction with Catholic children, most of whom went to the parochial school on the other side of town.

Though my own best friend during those years was Catholic, he and I were far more interested in roaming about the woods behind his home and riding our bikes than discussing theology.

Indeed, some of my first intimations of the considerable difference between what Catholics believed and what my faith tradition taught only began to hit me toward junior high school. I read a great deal, though taking on some of the classics of Western literature at age twelve meant that I didn't always understand what I was so voraciously reading. For some reason, I picked up Mary McCarthy's *Memories of a Catholic Girlhood,* and I do believe it was from there that I first encountered the terms "Assumption of Mary" and the "Immaculate Conception." I now have to laugh at myself a little, since, along with many Catholics, erroneously, I presumed the dogma of the Immaculate Conception referred to Jesus' sinlessness rather than Mary's own conception, which didn't really go against the grain of what we had been taught in Sunday school. But without any other information to go on, my own quick mind must have decided that the Assumption of Mary was a sort of Catholic philosophical concept that signified the way in which Mary made the assumption that Jesus was God in her own mind. To put it mildly, I was confused.

Not that I spent my high school years especially disturbed by things like the real meaning of Catholic dogmatic formulation. I was busy doing the things that high-school boys do — learning French, having crushes on my teachers, joining clubs — so it wasn't until my first year at a Catholic university that I encountered some of the famous paintings of the Assumption. For the life of me I couldn't figure out what an ecstatic Virgin Mary, hands raised to heaven amidst swirling blue and white angels, had to do with her belief in her own son's divinity. So I did what any bookish freshman might do: I hit the library.

Imagine my surprise when I learned what the dogma actually referred to, Mary herself being assumed bodily into heaven as an anticipation of the rapture for all of us! I continued to read Catholic theology that semester on my own, over and above the required course on theology, which was focused on spiritual autobiography and very little on the byways of dogmatic formulations. Mostly on my own, I learned a great deal. I didn't quite know what people like my father or mother would think about what appeared to me as an almost unsalubrious attention to bodily processes – virginity, birth, conception, incorruptibility, death – a lot of which made me squeamish. But the mysteriousness of these dogmas was definitely intriguing, and the amazing sensuality of the Catholic liturgy began to make more sense.

The process by which I was eventually received into the Church is a long story, and much of it directly attributable to the intercession of the Blessed Virgin Mary, who has always been acting in her low-key way behind the scenes. Nevertheless, her assumption into heaven has been an aspect of her life that until a couple of years ago I couldn't really find my way into making personal for myself, despite years of praying the rosary. I feel I have experienced certain kinds of resurrections and ascensions in my life, and most certainly have had the Spirit of God come upon me, but being assumed bodily into heaven wasn't even something I was able to make my own, spiritually speaking.

However, one year during Lent, for reasons completely unknown to me my prayer life took a decided and dramatic turn down to another level of depth. I began to experience that deep interior silence that I had always read about in the lives of the mystics, felt myself wholly and fully absorbed into God's presence, especially after receiving the Eucharist, which at times felt like a trapdoor had opened out from under me and I would "come to" some time later, often finding myself alone in the church. I had undertaken a regime of somewhat rigorous fasting — one single small meal a day — which I have no doubt contributed to my inward deepening, but mostly I see that time as a special grace given to me for a purpose that has not yet, even now, been fully revealed.

In any case, I entered a prolonged state of consolation that Lent, the longest I have ever experienced, and the climax of it came after communion on a very short weekend retreat I took at a local monastery. I was already reverberating with the presence of Christ, feeling drenched in him, as if he permeated my whole body and soul. Rapt with attention in prayer before the tabernacle in the private chapel, I felt my soul leave my body, as if all the heaviness of my physical self were being gently left behind, and my true self was being drawn upward. I looked back and I could see myself from above, kneeling, joyous but utterly motionless, and continued to feel drawn upward very slowly and gently toward God. The sensation was definitely one of being drawn, as if my soul felt an attraction to the Divine and, by not resisting in any way, let itself move toward God. And yet I could feel my physical self as well. I could feel my arms outstretched, I could feel the weight of my legs. All the physical sensations I would have had I did have, but my earthly body was still before the tabernacle.

I don't know how long this experience lasted and at the end, I felt a large thumb imprint itself on my forehead, opening up a third eye of vision for me, and after a time, I felt myself descend again. The sensation of the third eye which came to me then lasted for quite a number of months, and often in mystical prayer I would very consciously employ that higher vision which was almost like a literal vision, enabling me to see things from just a slightly higher perspective than normal. It wasn't lost on me that the very place where I touched myself first with holy water in crossing myself was precisely where this visionary sight was located.

All of these mystical graces have faded over time for me, but they came to me at a time when, in his ineffable wisdom, God decided I needed them to confirm my faith and move me forward into another level of intimacy with Christ. So, now, I now have not just a picture but a profound interior experience of what Mary's assumption must have been like, what it will be like when we will be raised incorruptible. My closeness to her, already strong, has continued to grow, and through prayer, both mystical and ordinary, God's presence in the world and in my own body likewise continues to be revealed to me.

full of grace . . .

One of the keenest pleasures of being the longtime friend of a working visual artist is that birthdays, holidays, and special occasions are usually much anticipated: what sort of piece will Tanya be giving me? I remember when she was going about the world learning the various arcane techniques of making paper. I have been present for her years of experimentalism and trepidation at the first showings of her highly symbolic works of paper art, and in recent years, I have watched her artistic vision and technical skill deepen.

Some years before I became officially Catholic, she had given me for a birthday a perfectly delightful piece of work that she had entitled *Soror Mystica,* a reference to Jung which the two of us Jungian psychotherapists shared, as well as a lovely and touching comment on our friendship, too. Into a background of slightly iridescent brown paper, she had pressed a small white lace dress, the zippered back of it facing out, making it appear that the woman who had been occupying the dress had, miraculously, amazingly, unaccountably, been taken up into heaven in a flash, leaving only the dress behind to float gently back down to earth. If I remember correctly, I laid eyes on this piece and the first thing I said was, "Oops, where did she go?" I laughed and made a little "whoosh" gesture with my hand.

For the longest time after receiving this charming gift of art, it hung beside my bed: in earthquake-prone California, one dearly appreciates the beauty and functionality of paper art for the bedroom, lest one be killed by some falling frame or bronze statuette in the middle of a 8.0 quake. However, when my office building had a fire and I moved my tan leather furniture into a temporary space where I continued to see clients in the interim, the blank walls—and the somewhat ambivalent effect of my previous art work in the office on certain clients—made me think that this less provocative, somewhat whimsical piece of Tanya's would work better. For those nine months, the "mystic sister" hung there instead, and it was one evening, when saying the glorious mysteries of the rosary at the end of a long Wednesday night, I perceived that Tanya's piece was actually one of the more evocative representations of my own vision of the Assumption I had ever seen. The pink-cheeked angels, ecstatic gestures, and whirling cloud-masses of the Venetian school appealed to me, to be sure, but here, in the simplicity and mysteriousness of this empty white dress, was a far more apt image of Mary's physical movement from earth into heaven, a modern Assumption, unassuming, credible, enigmatic.

The piece has since moved back into my bedroom, and I have since become a confirmed Catholic, brought into the Church on Easter of the Jubilee Year, by the grace of the woman who does not appear in this work of art. Rather, her mystical presence and the remnant of her earthly existence, a petite faded white gown, faces me in the place where I meditate. She is no longer beside me, where I cannot see her, but instead, she is before me. I am happy to say that I have been given dispensation by the artist herself to understand this piece not simply as any old *soror mystica* but to own la Santa Madonna Assunta herself as the woman suggested here, my own mystical sister in faith. "The Assumption?" said Tanya, when I told her of my interpretation. "Sure, Mary works."

But art continually reveals something new, great art, at least, and Tanya's gift to me has led me to experience Mary as sister, not just as mother, virgin, or queen. This modern Assumption upon which I gaze during my nightly rosary has lent a special intimacy to my meditation upon the glorious mysteries. Indeed caring, devoted, nourishing, protective — in short — motherly, l'Assunta is also an older sister to us all, sharing our devotion and showing us, body and soul, the way into blessing and rest.

the Lord is with you.

Mary Brumley writes: "We speak of Mary's Assumption, not her Ascension. Christ ascended, but the Blessed Virgin Mary was assumed into heaven. In other words, unlike her Son Jesus, Mary didn't 'go up on her own power' to heaven, so to speak, but was taken up by the power of God. The Assumption of Mary, then, is something God did for her, like her Immaculate Conception and Virginal Motherhood, not something she did herself. It is a result of Christ's redemptive power applied to the Blessed Mother."

Unquestionably, Mary is the screen upon which generations of men and women have projected their own images of gender-related stereotypes and characteristics, so passages like the above, dry and academically straightforward as they are in explaining the traditional understanding of the Assumption, nevertheless cannot be neutral. We bring to such descriptions our own prejudices, experiences, and associations to what it means to be a man and what it means to be a woman, and to read such an explanation as this one, for me, is to read, "Men are active, women are passive. Men are the agents, women the patients."

Now I know from my two decades of psychotherapy work with Americans and from my life as a man on this earth, that passivity as a personality characteristic is in great disfavor among us. We are supposedly the heirs of a grand secular tradition of self-actualization, assertiveness training, and taking charge of our own manifest destiny. So the phobia concerning even the merest hint of passivity that currently afflicts men—and now postfeminist women—is quite understandable. Nevertheless, the passivity which many of Mary's mysteries represent, beginning with the receptiveness of the Annunciation, the ponderings of her heart and helpless witness of her son's Passion, and here, finally in the Assumption and the Coronation, in which she receives transformative graces, are not passivity in the ordinary sense. Indeed, as an individual, the Gospel writers go to great pains to present her as somewhat assertive in social situations, the quintessential Jewish mother. She reprimands her son in the temple, she tugs on his sleeve at Cana, she attends his public teaching, she is at the foot of the cross, she doesn't demur from taking her place as an apostle among the Apostles. For whatever sexist purposes her image has been used over the ages in a patriarchal culture to keep women in their place, the Gospels themselves do not present her as submissive.

Nor does the authentic tradition, I would argue. Mary's passivity is misunderstood when it is psychologized. The passivity we perceive in her stories actually represents a spiritual stance, a way of relating to God, not to men, and, as such, the stories that are the foundation for the rosary mysteries provide us all with a very powerful model of contemplative living. She is quite active in her relationship to other human beings, even at times a little pushy; it is only in regard to her Creator that she is "hand-maid." To misunderstand her passivity through psychosocial lenses and then to reject it out of hand as an anachronistic relic of sexist expectations is to miss the redemption of passivity in the realm of spirit which Mary and her image could bring to our relationship to the Source of our Being.

We did not bring ourselves into being. We receive life, and we receive it from a Source of Being that remains mysterious and incomprehensible. Mary urges us to make this awareness a basic attitude for going about our lives here on earth, and her mysteries disclose what flows from this awareness of our own contingency: humility, gratitude, confidence, faith, a joyous capacity to receive. This is her passivity, a spiritual attitude that gives birth to a host of virtues — countercultural virtues, to be sure, in a society stuck in largely adolescent issues of power and identity defined through often gratuitous rebellion and self-assertion. Thus the virtue of spiritual passivity is easily misunderstood or, worse, co-opted by the oppressive powers of this world. But that is not Mary's fault — that is ours. Her spiritual truth, her complete willingness throughout her life to be "taken up by God," continues to shine for us all the same.

Blessed are you among women...

The first time when I heard her voice, it startled me. I was in the middle of praying and just as clear as a bell, like she was standing right behind me, I heard to her say to me, "Have no fear. All is well." I even turned around to look at who said it, just to make sure I wasn't making things up. And for about seven days afterward, whenever I would pray the rosary, she repeated this to me, those words only: "Have no fear. All is well." That was her good counsel to me, and sometimes at work or at home when I get discouraged, I take a moment and remember what she said to me, and I feel much better, as though I can let go of my anxiety and trust in God's providence.

Another time, I was praying in a little chapel by the seashore where I sometimes go on vacation with my family, and I heard her say to me, "I want you for my son." I still haven't figured out what that one meant, and she hasn't ever said it again to me, so I am not clear if it was her way of telling me that I am called to religious life or whether she considers me her spiritual child. It could be taken in both ways. Nevertheless, I heard her say it very clearly in the empty chapel where I was praying that day, and I've never forgotten it. I suppose it seems from the outside that it would take great faith to believe that such statements did come from the Blessed Virgin Mary, but for me, it doesn't really take any faith at all. I know what I experienced, and I know it is her. It is not faith. It is certainty.

I sometimes wish people would take the time to pray more or use the rosary to open themselves up to the mysteries, because then I think many problems inside and out could then find the right solution or resolution. Prayer is really just listening, in my opinion, and I have gotten lots of good advice over the years. Lots of time the advice is simply not to do anything. We are all so used to intervening, managing, acting, especially in my field of social work, and what I have learned from my prayer life and from our Mother is sometimes situations will just resolve themselves. So many times I have been advised by her just to have faith and let the situation unfold. When working with certain families in conflict, that can be hard because I feel myself drawn into the conflict and want to take sides or confront certain family members. But I don't. I hold back and simply allow myself to be present to them all as they work it through, and so often they do. Or sometimes they don't, and that can be the best thing for everyone, too, because people need to move on or separate. I have learned that I don't always know best, and that I need to really let go of my ego and my professionalism and all that stuff and let God do his work in the world. This is a lesson I have learned from the Blessed Mother. If I can say it this way, it is my personal version of the Assumption: I let my own will and my own pride be assumed by God into his great plan for everyone. It is very humbling but also very freeing.

and blessed is the fruit of your womb, Jesus.

I was taught to use the mystery of the Assumption in the rosary to pray for the grace of a happy death, which, when I look back on it, was somewhat macabre to recommend as a meditation for a young person. Yet strangely, I didn't find it so. I came from a family where we used the second verse of "Away in a Manger" as a bedtime prayer:

> Be near me Lord Jesus, I ask thee to stay
> Close by me forever and love me, I pray.
> Bless all the dear children in Thy tender care
> And take us to heaven to live with Thee there.

We also prayed the "Now I Lay Me Down to Sleep" asking the Lord to take my soul "if I should die before I wake." So my associations to the Assumption are soothing and homey, and my childhood vision was that death was like Mary's, a simple floating up to heaven to be with Jesus.

My faith is why I do not have a terrible fear of death or a great distaste or grief around loved ones who have passed on. I truly believe that they have passed on, and that they continue toward full communion with God. I do not feel it is right for me to begrudge them that state of beatitude. Rather, I feel it is my obligation to pray for their progress, and many times I do feel they have interceded for me around certain situations and petitions, especially those related to our family. So I do take seriously Church teaching about belief in the communion of saints, and I believe that there are many saints beyond those who have been specifically canonized. I have known a few in my life, particularly my grandmother, who I have no doubt lived a very holy life and is certainly with God.

I use the Assumption to pray for the souls of departed loved ones on a regular basis, at least once a week. Because I had two sets of parents, both a stepmother and a stepfather, a single decade of the rosary allows me to pray for all eight grandparents, plus my deceased mother and father. I name each person on each bead by beginning "For the soul of Maria Grazia" or "Pasquale" or "Alma," and so forth, before beginning the individual Hail Marys. I have had a number of friends, acquaintances, and co-workers also pass on, some in a very difficult way, unreconciled with family or by their own hand, and so I make a point of regularly praying for them during my rosary prayers on the Assumption, because I fear their souls may be not at rest and that in the afterlife they need our help and goodwill to open themselves to the infinite love of God in a way they could not during their life here on earth. Our parish uses the Fatima prayer in communal rosary recitation, and these are the people I pray for, those souls most in need of God's mercy. I also occasionally dedicate the decade for those who have no one to pray for the eternal rest of their souls, people who have died unmourned without loved ones. During November, the month of the Holy Souls, I do this every time I pray the Assumption on my rosary. As I said, I feel the presence and intercession of those who have returned to God very strongly, and my prayers are a way to return some of that love.

Holy Mary...

My first experience with the rosary as a non-Catholic was at St. Anthony's Hospital in Amarillo, Texas. My family had taken me many places, including St. Louis, looking for a specialist to operate on an eye problem. But the Lord brought us back to a hospital within fifty miles of home. My eyes were covered with huge bandages after the operation, and though I was only six years old, I tried very, very hard to be brave. I could not see but I heard people walking up and down the halls. Mingled with their soft, happy voices, there was a whisper of long skirts and beads clicking, as if playing together. "Happy talk," I thought as this gentle, reassuring symphony of sound would enter my room. The wonderful ladies who wore long, white skirts and wooden beadsongs turned out to be Catholic nuns. At the time, I had no idea what a nun—or a rosary, or a Catholic—was, but knew whatever it all meant, I wanted to be a part of it forever. I knew it had to do with Jesus, and my mom had given me a little prayer to say to Jesus when I was afraid.

After I became a Catholic fifteen years later, the rosary still was not a part of my prayer life, but I did love beads. I was delighted to discover the root word for bead, *bede*, meant "to pray" and I would share this with my students while teaching contemporary and traditional beading techniques in workshops for national conferences and in universities throughout the U.S.

Before Peter, my husband of thirty-nine years, died from a long and very difficult bout with cancer, I took up the rosary with intensity. I promised the Blessed Mother to pray the rosary every day for the rest of my life, regardless of the outcome of his illness, and during this time, Mary taught me much about the power of the prayer bead. She has never stopped.

Thirty years ago, I had bought a bag of wonderful, old, mismatched wooden beads from a San Diego bead dealer, and strung them on a cord to make a rosary out of them. Over the years of seven children and many moves, this first rosary I made got broken, dismantled, and ended up in a little plastic sandwich bag stored away. Only a few years ago did the bag resurface and, like putting my life back together again after Peter's death, I took those old mismatched beads and restrung them back into a rosary again. As I did, the aroma of those old wooden hall floors soaked with oily preservatives in St. Anthony Hospital came back. Once again, I heard the beadsong: first the foot steps, then the lilt of soft, happy voices mingled with long, swishing skirts, and dancing wooden beads that drew me to the Lord.

Mother of God . . .

In these days when so many good parents have children who have lost their faith, I have come to feel, through my experience with my own mother, that praying the rosary is one very important way to help our children return to an active faith. Though my mother never saw the results of her prayers while on earth, my siblings and I are sure her prayers are even more powerful now that she is with Our Lord. You see, my mother was the mother of nine, eight of whom were still living when she died, but at the time only two of us were still active in our practice of the faith. For this reason, she said four or five rosaries every day, mostly for her children to return to the faith.

For the last twenty-four years of her life, she lived with me, and at the age of eighty-six, she begun to have a series of strokes, receiving last rites several times during her final three-month illness. All during the day of August 30, she lay in a semi-comatose state and was on oxygen, and in the early morning hours of August 31, I heard her breathing become more labored. After making her as comfortable as I could, I lay my head next to her and whispered three Hail Marys. In the only movement she had made for about twenty-four hours, she turned her eyes to me. I asked her if she wanted me to say the whole rosary and she blinked her eyes. I said the rosary and as soon as I finished it, she smiled, looked up in the corner, and breathed her last.

Since her death, however, her prayers on behalf of her family have become so much more powerful: quite unexpectedly, six of my siblings have returned to the faith, so now my mother only has the two youngest, twins, to get back to God. We believe her devotion to the rosary and her intercession are behind much of what has happened in the faith lives of her children. Not wanting to presume she is in heaven, we all still keep praying for the repose of her soul. After all, prayers are never wasted, are they?

pray for us sinners now . . .

Most of my locutions are for my own education, but Our Lady told me something one time that I am allowed to share with people. Not that she forbade it, but she preferred that people not be buried with their rosary. She said, "The dead cannot pray the rosary. Every rosary that is left unsaid is a triumph for the Evil One." Rather than burying the rosary with the person, she told me that it should be displayed and then given to someone for whom the rosary would really mean something. She said, however, that it's okay to bury the dead with something that looks like a rosary, for example, an arrangement of real rosebuds, which, after all, isn't something you can use to really pray with. Bury something beautiful but not practical, such as a natural thing. She thinks that the rosary is something that should be used. So now I try to steer people away from the practice of burying their rosaries, though I do know that many of the rosaries I have made are now buried. However, if it gives comfort to someone, Our Lady is fully aware of that.

and at the hour of our death.

I have come to spontaneously associate the rosary mysteries with the seasons of the year, roughly corresponding to the liturgical calendar: winter and early spring seem to be the season of the Joyous Mysteries — everything in quiet renewal, waiting to burst out and begin growing. Late spring and early summer, fertile as Palm Sunday and punishingly hot and dry as the Passion, is the time of the Sorrowful Mysteries. And late summer/harvest-time the season of the Glorious Mysteries.

I wonder if the Feast of the Assumption in August was intentionally placed at a time of year when all comes to fruition and must be cut down, stored up, and consumed. If there was no conscious intention, then there was certainly a kind of divinely inspired collective wisdom behind the decision, in my opinion. Autumn is the culmination of the year for me, especially where I live, when the natural world is especially glorious in color. It's a time of incredible satisfaction. It is the end of the old and the beginning of the new, fullness of redemption leading into a time of withdrawal and simplicity. The round-and-roundness of the rosary mysteries have for many years helped me to stay in touch with these cycles, which seem to me to invite an especially feminine awareness. I bring that sense of the seasons to Mary when I spend time with her in prayer, as well as my gratitude for what she knew of God's eternal cycles of life and death, and her willingness to share what she lived with all of us through her son.

Amen.

Coronation of Mary

All, according to their state, should strive to bring alive the wondrous virtues of our heavenly Queen and most loving Mother through constant effort of mind and manner. Thus will it come about that all Christians, in honoring and imitating their sublime Queen and Mother, will realize they are truly brothers, and with all envy and avarice thrust aside, will promote love among classes, respect the rights of the weak, cherish peace. No one should think himself a son of Mary, worthy of being received under her powerful protection, unless, like her, he is just, gentle and pure, and shows a sincere desire for true brotherhood, not harming or injuring but rather helping and comforting others. (Pope Pius XII)

Hail, Mary...

On days when I am home, I always intend to get to my rosary early in the day, but I usually end up only having the time and mental space by late afternoon. Dinner is in the oven or on the stove, my partner isn't home yet, and I can't really start any new housekeeping or gardening projects, so the rosary at sunset is like my form of evening prayer. I light a candle by the small Christmas card of Madonna and Child I got from a friend last year and had framed, settle in on the couch, and I take some time in silence to put a close to the events of the day and to anticipate what tomorrow may bring. Both of these things are important for me to do on a regular basis to maintain a spiritual balance in my life: let go of the past and look forward with hope and faith to the future.

I ask Mary to help me with putting aside what I have done and what I left undone in the day: when I have been impatient while driving, when I could have been more sensitive, or conversely, rejoice in the little bit of good I may have or feel gratitude for the opportunity to minister or witness. I often bring these concerns to my contemplation of the Sorrowful Mysteries, since they have a penitential feel to me. However, I also feel it is equally appropriate to ask Mary to help me look forward to the next day or week or month, my best friend's birthday party that we're going to be a part of weekend after next, my niece and nephew's second baby due in a month or so, the workshop I've committed to give in December. The Gospel is good news, so I make sure I call upon the Blessed Mother to help me rejoice with her in anticipation of blessings. These thoughts, hopes, and dreams even, are the humble "glorious mysteries" of my own life, things which I look forward to. It would be very easy to let the darkness of my everyday limits and failings overcome the light in my life, so the rosary of Our Lady is a way to keep myself balanced. She is my bright light, reflecting Christ's joy and peace, promise and hope.

full of grace...

I didn't really know much about the rosary at the beginning of my rosary-making—just the prayers and a few memories. So as my relationship to the rosary deepened, I decided to research the history, traditions, and craft of it. Knowing more about the origins of this form of prayer couldn't help but enhance my awareness, though like all subjects theological and spiritual, I was a bit amazed at the real history of the devotion and the various legends and myths. I guess some people might find this distinction disturbing. For me, it is the opposite: the idea that the rosary has its origin not in some medieval miracle but rather in the ancient prayer cords of the desert fathers grounds my rosary-praying even more.

Inspired by the many lovely rosary-makers I have encountered, both online and in person, I began to collect rosaries and found that each set of beads I got seemed to have its own spirit, purpose, and effect on my prayer life. After obtaining a few dozen, I naturally had to begin trying my hand at making them. The first couple were "interesting," which is to say not especially durable, but then I got some advice from some of the older and wiser rosary-ladies online and sure enough, I began to hit my stride, ferreting out sources for older-style parts, unusual beads, haunting various secondhand stores with some older necklaces ready to be restrung with sacred intention. Eventually, as my Tupperware bucket of finished rosaries began to overflow, I discovered how seductive the rosary is: various friends of mine, some Catholic, some not, some of whom are distinctly antireligion, nevertheless were quite taken with the beauty and functionality of them and got bitten by the same bug as I had — collecting them, loving to hold them and feel them. Many of them started praying with them, not always using the traditional prayers, of course, but I don't think that really matters. I think the Blessed Mother has room in her lap for all who thirst to know and love God.

I try not to think about the powerful effect my rosaries may have on the lives of others. It's too awesome to think that I, with my little bead-stringing habit, might in this modest way be an instrument of God's grace, but of course I am, so I suppose I should get used to it. The older and wiser rosary-makers I know have accepted their part with grace and thanksgiving, and I suppose, in time, I will, too. I thank the Lord every day for the gift of this devotion and for those who gave me the beauty of their own craft and the love of Mary behind it—they have indeed been the means of God's plan for me.

the Lord is with you.

Imagine telling a little boy whose dad made him a beautiful rosary for his first communion that wearing it in devotion is a "sin"! Talk about wrong-headed teaching! However well-intentioned she may have been in making sure that the kids understood the true purpose of a rosary, I must respectfully disagree with her.

I wear my rosaries all the time—indeed I never leave home without one around my neck, tucked into my shirt—but some people I know have been raised with the opposite custom, that demoting the rosary to just another piece of jewelry is disrespectful, even sinful. Wasn't that part of Madonna's "shock" effect in her music video, draping herself with rosaries as she gyrated in leather and lace to the boom-boom-boom of "Like a Virgin," a rebellion against the pious folkways of her Italian-American culture? So, as always, there is capital-T Tradition and little-t traditions or customs.

If a "sin" is anything that separates us from God, then it all comes down to the purpose of wearing a rosary, doesn't it? Speaking for myself, wearing my rosary brings me closer to God, reminds me that at all times and in all situations that I am a witness to my faith. It is a visible symbol of my commitment to model my life and my actions on Christ. Isn't this why we wear any form of ritual jewelry or clothing—a wedding ring, a cross, a veil? Members of various religious orders wear their fifteen-decade rosaries as a part of their habit for the same reason — hardly a sin, indeed, the opposite of a sin, an outward sign of faith.

Is it possible that issues of masculinity and femininity contributed to the teacher's overreaction — seeing a little boy wearing a "necklace," a piece of devotional jewelry often perceived as a part of "feminine" devotion? Having grown up with a plethora of interests and tastes that weren't conventionally masculine, I feel for those boys whose devotion to Mary is looked at with such narrow-mindedness. What a shame, it seems to me, that such devotion, even to the point of wearing a rosary, would be discouraged among young men for these sexist reasons.

Blessed are you among women . . .

> Queen of saints and angels
> But not a Queen on throne
> So far above us
> But gentle Queen of Love
> Now in Heaven
> Fold us in your mantle,
> Not of silk and velvet,
> But the mantle of your love

and blessed is the fruit of your womb, Jesus.

Scott Hahn writes: "Too many Catholics and Orthodox Christians have abandoned their rich heritage of Marian devotions. They've been cowed by the polemics of fundamentalists, shamed by the snickering of dissenting theologians, or made sheepish by well-meaning but misguided ecumenical sensitivities. They're happy to have a mom who prays for them, prepares their meals and keeps their home; they just wish she'd stay safely out of sight when others are around who 'just wouldn't understand.'

"I too have been guilty of this filial neglect—not only with my earthly mother, but also with my mother in Jesus Christ, the Blessed Virgin Mary. The path of my conversion led me from juvenile delinquency to Presbyterian ministry. All along the way, I had my anti-Marian moments.

"My earliest encounter with Marian devotion came when my Grandma Hahn died. She'd been the only Catholic on either side of my family, a quiet, humble, and holy soul. Since I was the only 'religious' one in the family, my father gave me her religious articles when she died. I looked at them with horror. I held her rosary in my hands and ripped it apart, saying, 'God, set her free from the chains of Catholicism that have bound her.' I meant it, too. I saw the rosary and the Virgin Mary as obstacles that came between Grandma and Jesus Christ.

"Even as I slowly approached the Catholic faith—drawn inexorably by the truth of one doctrine after another—I could not make myself accept the Church's Marian teaching.

"The proof of her maternity would only come, for me, when I made the decision to let myself be her son. Despite all the powerful scruples of my Protestant training — remember, just a few years before, I had torn apart my Grandma's beads — I took up the rosary one day and began to pray. I prayed for a very personal, seemingly impossible intention. On the next day, I took up the beads again, and the next day and the next. Months passed before I realized that my intention, the seemingly impossible situation, had been reversed since the day I first prayed the rosary. My petition had been granted.

"From that moment, I knew my mother. From that moment, I believe, I truly knew my home in the covenant family of God: Yes, Christ was my brother. Yes, He'd taught me to pray 'Our

Father.' Now, in my heart, I accepted His command to behold *my* mother."

Holy Mary...

When I pray the rosary—and I like the word "pray" not "say"—I take a title of Mary from the Litany of the Blessed Virgin Mary, and simply pray it on all beads, depending on what I need. If I need wisdom, I pray, "Mary, Seat of Wisdom, pray for me" or, if one day I feel particularly joyless, I pray, "Mary, cause of our joy, pray for me." This is just so utterly simple, but it works for me.

Mother of God...

I also have made a practice of modifying the Hail Mary for the mystery of the Coronation, adding a particular virtue of Mary to the first phrase of the Ave, for each one of the ten beads. For example, "Hail, Mary, full of grace and humility," "Hail, Mary, full of grace and charity," "Hail, Mary, full of grace and joy," bringing to mind in a rough kind of order the various qualities she exemplified as summed up in the rosary mysteries. "Hail, Mary, full of grace and obedience," "Hail, Mary, full of grace and endurance," "Hail, Mary, full of grace and strength in suffering." She responded to the various circumstances of her earthly life and her motherhood of God in ways the rosary is meant to help us emulate, so it struck me as appropriate to use the final mystery as a way to hold them all together. If she is so often portrayed as being crowned with stars by Christ, then each of those stars is a special virtue of hers, no? "Hail, Mary, full of grace and unquestioning faith," "Hail, Mary, full of grace and apostolic zeal," "Hail, Mary, full of grace, model of contemplation," "Hail, Mary, full of grace and united with Christ, the Lord is with thee."

I haven't yet gotten the courage to insert these phrases into the communal rosary we say at my parish, but one day I will when it feels right and the Spirit is with me. I have a feeling that people would think about that final mystery differently if they prayed this way. I know it makes me feel much closer to Mary, to think so specifically about who she was as a person, what kind of qualities she brought to bear on her life. As Queen of Heaven she seems so far away, so abstract, so maybe I just need something like these little phrases to make her less regal and more human. I hope she doesn't mind.

pray for us sinners now...

There is more to being an instrument of the Lord's peace by doing things—whether in the world at large, in the local community, in schools or at home. I believe that you can also be an instrument of the Lord's peace by *not* doing things. You can be a peacemaker by *not* spreading hate and violence toward our enemies, toward people of other races.

I feel I do my part in being a peacemaker in this world by praying the rosary. So many things that need to be done to bring peace to the world are out of reach for most of us. However, the one thing that is within the reach of anyone is prayer. So I pray the rosary for peace. I mourn those whose lives have been lost in war and violence. I pray for all the families who suffer because of these deaths. I walk with Mary, turn to Mary for comfort. For if anyone can bring peace to our country and families, it is the Queen of Peace, the Blessed Mother. Nothing feels better than the warm sensitivity of a mother's care.

The rosary began in a time when conditions were the same as today—men involved in wars, fighting for their rights and beliefs. Today, we are faced with similar situations, and it is clear to me that this is certainly a time when we need Mary the most, she whom God prepared to be the understanding mother of all mankind. Praying to Mary can only result in good things for all of us.

and at the hour of our death.

I did manage to refrain from being too overtly miffed at finding the canvas rolled up in a careless kind of way and stuffed behind a huge dusty pile of painted ostrich eggs in the shop by my office. The shop is a quirky little place, after all, full of antique *objets d'art decoratifs,* many of which have a nineteenth-century Catholic flavor to them, not unlike a campy, self-conscious re-creation of what any of us might be afraid to find in the attic of a pious great-aunt after her death. I couldn't help, though, feeling slightly piqued at this rather opulent oil painting of Our Lady of the Rosary, painted, I was told, by a modern Peruvian in imitation of an older style. It was well done, even if unnecessarily creased and abraded. The artist had chosen a quite convincing patina, dark sepia for the background and a wealth of very fine, gold-leaf detail carefully applied to her rich crown and crimson gown and to the Christ-child's rosy garment. She looked regal, holding the little Prince of Peace in her left arm, light as a feather, and she dangled a tiny pearl rosary off the fingers of her right hand. Seeing her image treated with unintended disrespect was like finding someone having tossed pictures of your family into the recycling bin at work. For a mere hundred bucks, she was mine, to be added to my collection of Marys, and for the time being, I knew I had no place to display her.

Enthused by finding her and admittedly, a little nutty with affection for the Blessed Mother, I didn't actually look at the whole of the painting, focusing mostly on her noble expression and the sweet solemnity of Jesus holding his hand up in blessing. I rolled it out on the table at the frame shop and the woman helping me exclaimed, "What an unusual piece!" I told her a bit of the story, how I found it and what I wanted to do—crown it with a gold frame, not too grand, but not too mousy, either.

The image had caught her, that I could see, and I knew that expression—affectionate, intrigued, seduced by the grace and the power of her. She stared and smiled. "So what are all these symbols?"

It was my turn to be startled. I hadn't noticed them before, but the artist had surrounded the figure with representations of Mary's titles. "Well, this one is easy." I pointed to the large pink rose down in the right corner. "Mary is called the Mystic Rose for her beauty and delicacy."

"And this one?" She pointed at a gold representation of a church in the upper right.

"House of Gold, I assume." I looked up. "She is a precious container of faith, both her faith and our own. And here," I pointed to a large mirror painted on her right side. "This is Mary as Mirror of Justice. Her compassion mirrors the righteousness of Christ her son to the world." I hoped I wasn't being too out-there with the Mary witness here in this frame shop, but heck, I'm a Mary guy and I really don't much care who knows about it. Can anyone really fault a man in love?

"Wow," she said under her breath, still looking at the canvas. "Many titles."

I mused further, examining what looked like a wall of gold bricks drawn high on the left. "This must represent the wall of the temple. She is known as the Temple of the Holy Spirit, since by the Spirit of God, she became the mother of Jesus. You are right, she has many titles."

"You know, my daughter is very interested in Mary," she said to me. "I don't think she knows all these things about her in Catholic tradition. Mary has other titles, then?"

"Oh yes. In fact, there is a whole litany of them we recite. I especially like this one little sequence, Health of the Infirm, Refuge of Sinners, Consolation of the Afflicted, Help of Christians."

"Refuge of Sinners?" She looked at me, smiling, but I could perceive something in her eyes, something I dared not mention. "That is very comforting. Refuge of Sinners." She looked down again at the canvas and her gaze softened. "Imagine her being a refuge. That is very beautiful."

I could say that I don't know what possessed me, but I do. I reached into my shoulder bag and pulled out a small gold Miraculous Medal, one of three I had just picked up the day before at one of the local religious arts stores for tiny ivory confirmation rosaries I was preparing to make. "Here you go. This is a medal of Mary. Wear it if you need protection or refuge."

She did not hesitate. "My daughter will want to know where I got this," and with that, she undid a long chain around her neck and slipped the medal on it, patting it and smiling. "I don't think about sin much, but I guess this'll cover me, huh?"

"Source of our joy. *Fonte della nostra gioia*," I replied, pointing to the fountain on the right. "I think of her as the sum total of every mother's love for every child that has ever been. She is the best mother in the world, and she loves all her children. So, yes, in her hands, I think you're covered. Just say a prayer now and then, and she'll be listening."

Amen.

Salve

I have been so absorbed in the light from the monstrance, losing myself in the vision of its reflection on the chapel floor, that I have come to the end of my rosary after what feels like only a few moments before the Blessed Sacrament. In this loving presence beyond time, my fingers have found their way back to the cool bronze center, and the feel of the engraved image of Mary against the tip of my index finger brings me back to this world, familiar, yes, but also strange. Most of the brothers have gathered by now, and quite a few of the regular guests as well, and I see that the tall candlesticks have been placed at the ends of the pews, already lit, flickering happily, waiting patiently.

I breathe deeply, smelling the last of the incense, and I come back more fully to where I belong for now, this realm of space and time. Father Dominic makes his way slowly toward the altar until, with a gesture so tenderly paternal and reverent it makes me want to cry, he gathers up the Host with the folds of his scapular. For a few moments longer, we all tacitly agree to hold the silence, stay motionless and peaceful, until the contemplative mood is at last broken at the closing click of the tabernacle. Lights go on, to our feet we shuffle, and I put my amber rosary around my neck, warm against my chest.

Were I alone, I would have already said the final prayer in honor of Mary's majesty and compassion, the Salve I have come to love, but on Sunday night here in the priory, Night Prayer after Eucharistic Adoration ends with a communal procession by candlelight out to the central courtyard, singing the Gregorian setting of this traditional prayer with a single voice. Instead, I use this ritual to end my rosary prayer for the day, bringing Sunday to a close and marking the beginning of a new week.

Hail, we say in English, reproducing the very association as in the original Latin *salve,* both words growing out of that common loving wish of human beings to be instruments of wholeness one to another. To be hale is to be healthy, to be hailed is to be greeted with a wish for health. A desire for salvation animates the sinuous first phrase of our Salve, lilting, bittersweet, and in me, this flame burns bright against a cold, dark winter evening.

> *Salve, regina!*
> Save us, sweet Mother of us all!

Our song moves out of the chapel, resounding in the confines of the hallway, the melody unbroken, each of us sharing one breath and one spirit, each of us fervent and sensitive to do her honor with the best of our voices. We emerge into the cloister, past the bell, past the birds, past the crimson bougainvillea and the intoxicating night-blooming jasmine, our praise joining the music of the plashing water in the fishpond. Over the profound silence of individual experience, our song glides light and strong as beading wire, drawing every one of us together into a single line, a circle, a community, a church.

> Salve and soothe us, source of spiritual life!
> Make our reverence truly salutary, *salve!*

Before Mary's tall white figure at the end of the walkway, we stop and stand beside one another, laypeople and brothers, priests and sisters, women and men, young and old, guests and residents, and for one final time, we draw in breath as one. I never want this *salve* to end, always imagine how it would be to feel my soul borne up forever on the swells of this ancient, yearning prayer, but here we are in the realm of the senses, time bound with rhyme and meter, lives punctuated with sighs and tears. Wisely or foolishly, even the deepest breath we take must be spent, so onward we sing, accepting the inevitable and commending the homecoming of our soul, as Mary did, to the grace of God.

> In your virtues may we find our way to the son you held in
>   your body.
> In your arms and in your soul, our wholeness, your Jesus!
> In your compassion, his all-forgiving embrace.
> In your faithfulness, his sure promise.
> In your tenderness, his redemption.

The sky is clear, black as garnet, and the moon rises pale but enormous over the brick gables of the house. Once we offer her name, *Maria,* up to the fullness of the evening, our prayer gives way to stillness, a gracious, luminous stillness from which all has come and to which all will, we believe, eventually return. In that light, we stand for a time together before her, wondering, silent, grateful.

Entering into the Mysteries of Light

In October 2002, Pope John Paul II celebrated the twenty-fourth anniversary of his pontificate by declaring a Year of the Rosary until October 2003 and making the first significant change to the rosary in centuries by recommending that the faithful add a fourth set of mysteries, the Mysteries of Light, to the traditional Joyful, Sorrowful, and Glorious mysteries as a focus for meditation and prayer. For a devotion as longstanding as the rosary and one historically tied to lay spirituality, this innovative approach to the renewal of the rosary took many Catholics by surprise, challenging some, disconcerting others, delighting most.

There is no reasonable way to imagine that this newer set of mysteries would instantaneously attain the depth and resonance that the traditional mysteries have had for those of us who have been praying the rosary for years, if not our whole lives. However, as all the foregoing stories and reflections from the real lives of people demonstrate, the rosary devotion is quite alive in the hearts and minds of the people of God, and, as a living devotion, it is capable of growing, changing, expanding, perhaps even transcending itself. By taking the living essence of the rosary prayer seriously and suggesting the contemplation of episodes from Christ's prophetic and public ministry, the Holy Father has brought the rosary's timeless beauty into the third millennium.

From conversations with fellow rosary-prayers and rosary-makers, from careful reading and meditation upon the pope's apostolic letter *Rosarium virginis Mariae* but mostly from "living the mysteries" myself over these past months, I offer here my own reflections on how to enter the new Mysteries of Light so as to deepen our intimacy with Christ through Mary.

When to Pray the Mysteries of Light

For regular rosary-prayers, probably the first question that came to mind concerning five new mysteries was "when?" Creatures of habit we may well be, the consistency of the Monday-Wednesday, Thursday-Saturday cycle has been comforting to us all, mirroring in its consistency an infinite and unchangeable Presence behind the seasons of our mortal lives.

So now what? Where do we put the new Mysteries of Light in the course of our seven-day week? The Holy Father's own suggestion is, in essence, to consider the Mysteries of Light as an alternate beginning to the rosary cycle. Because both the Joyful Mysteries and the Mysteries of Light focus our attention to the two different "beginnings" experienced by Jesus—his early life on earth and the initiation of his public ministry, respectively— John Paul II has made the suggestion that the Mysteries of Light might be best used as a focus of prayer on Thursday. This suggestion leaves Monday-Tuesday-Wednesday for the traditional cycle, beginning with the Annunciation, and inaugurates the customary Thursday-Friday-Saturday cycle with meditation upon the start of Christ's public ministry at his Baptism in the Jordan. Because of a long-standing practice of devoting Saturday to Mary, the pope suggests in his apostolic letter that the faithful might also use Saturday as a time to meditate upon the Joyful Mysteries of the rosary.

Over the months of my own rosary meditations, in following the pope's recommendations, I have discovered that this new way of dedicating the days to each set of mysteries has renewed and refreshed my prayer life with the beads. The beginning of the week concentrates on the "historical" cycle of Jesus' life — starting with his conception and birth—while the latter part of the week imparts a more "thematic" perspective on the meaning and purpose of Christ's life on earth—revealing himself to us all through his actions as light of the world. To begin the rosary cycle with the Mysteries of Light has lent the Sorrowful and Glorious Mysteries a very different tone on the following days. To me, following contemplation of Christ as light, the events of the Sorrowful Mysteries are less shocking and tragic, flowing directly, naturally, out of the prophetic character of his call. The smoother association of the two has been an antidote against my own self-pity and murmuring when the Lord calls me to perform service in difficult circumstances. Similarly, I've found the new mysteries provide for a "big-picture" perspective, and this larger sweep of events has functioned to turn the whole week, rather than any single day, into the organizing principle behind my contemplative practice with the beads.

Two other ways of including the Mysteries of Light have also occurred spontaneously to me over the past few months. The first is to pray both the Joyful Mysteries and the Mysteries of Light on Mondays and Thursdays, thus preserving the well-worn groove of weekly habit and chronological order while at the same time gradually increasing time spent in prayer. For those of us who have the time and inclination, two sets of mysteries are indeed better than one.

Another practice I have been inspired to use is to pray on the Mysteries of Light as a special set of prayers before or after my own ministerial obligations at any time during the week. I have used the Mysteries of Light on Tuesday morning before I begin seeing clients as a way to consecrate my workweek to the Lord, or on Saturday following morning Mass as a way to enter into the proper frame of mind for doing spiritual direction later that day. By taking me through Christ's baptism in the Spirit and his acts of mercy, forgiveness, compassion, healing, and teaching, these mysteries are especially helpful to me in reminding me that it is the Spirit that works in and through me in my service to others. They focus my attention on how I might be the bringer of light, healing, and spiritual nourishment in *persona Christi,* in the place of Christ, with Mother Mary by my side.

The Mysteries of Light

Prayer is, as many wise women and men have said over the years, primarily *intention.* God, the all-knowing source of our very life, does not need us to tell him what we need, but we need to voice these needs, thoughts, wishes, and intentions to *ourselves* in the presence of the Lord, to make *ourselves* more aware of who we are in relationship to God.

The newer Mysteries of Light are, like nearly all the traditional mysteries of the rosary, drawn directly from scriptural sources, and so, the most direct fashion to weave them into our souls is to read the Gospel stories where these events in Jesus' life are most fully described. In the guide that follows, therefore, I lean upon Scripture in the way that Christians always have: to ground, to inspire, to draw us closer, to open our hearts, minds, and souls to the Word made flesh.

Because I cannot offer all the rich experiences of many years of contemplation upon these newer mysteries, what I give here instead — perhaps providentially — are *questions*. From decades of work as a psychotherapist, pastoral counselor, and spiritual director, I do know that asking the right question can at times be far more illuminating than my handing out the "right" answer to a client or directee. Reading about the spiritual experiences of others can be a bit of a passive experience, even for the most responsible and well-intentioned seeker after wisdom, and so this final section of "living the mysteries" feels like an apt way to end a book on the contemporary life of the rosary.

You, the reader, are now required to write the final chapter. Take the beads in your hand, let the Word of God in Scripture come into and through you, and begin your own journey through the questions that the Mysteries of Light ask of us all.

First Mystery: Jesus' Baptism in the Jordan (Matthew 3)

1. In those days came John the Baptist, preaching in the wilderness of Judea. "Repent, for the kingdom of heaven is at hand."

   Where is the wilderness in my life and do I feel God calling me to witness or repent?

2. Then went out to him Jerusalem and all Judea and all the region about the Jordan, and they were baptized by him in the river Jordan, confessing their sins.

   Where do I need to feel the cleansing spirit of God come upon me in my life, inside or outside? What is it I feel moved to confess?

3. He said to them… "I baptize you with water for repentance but he who is coming after me is mightier than I, whose sandals I am not worthy to carry; he will baptize you with the Holy Spirit and with fire."

How do I feel my own baptism at work in my life these days? Is it a baptism by water or by fire?

4. Then Jesus came from Galilee to the Jordan to John, to be baptized by him. John would have prevented him saying, "I need to be baptized by you, and do you come to me?"

Whose holiness has been a humbling inspiration for me? What blessings do I wish for her or him?

5. But Jesus answered him, "Let it be so now; for thus it is fitting for us to fulfil all righteousness."

Are there areas in my personal, professional, or spiritual life that I could use some patience to endure? What rituals help me do this?

6. And when Jesus was baptized, he went up immediately from the water and behold the heavens were opened.…

Who do I know who could use some help in emerging into the light of heaven from beneath a flood of worldly concerns, cares or trials?

7. And he saw the Spirit of God descending like a dove, and alighting on him.

How is the subtle presence of God hovering around me in ways I might be overlooking?

8. And lo, a voice from heaven, saying, "This is my beloved Son, with whom I am well pleased."

Are there particular situations in which I would like God's help to remember that I, too, am a child of God, pleasing and wonderfully made?

9. Then Jesus was led up by the Spirit into the wilderness, to be tempted by the devil.

   What are my temptations, and how might the Spirit be using them to enlighten me or others around me?

10. And he fasted forty days and forty nights.

    From what—literally or symbolically—could I profitably fast today?

Second Mystery: Jesus at the Wedding in Cana (John 2:1–12)

1. On the third day there was a marriage at Cana in Galilee, and the mother of Jesus was there.

   How does Mary stand with me right now in prayer? What does her presence feel like?

2. Jesus was also invited to the marriage, with his disciples.

   Are there couples and families I know who could use my prayers of celebration and blessing?

3. When the wine gave out, the mother of Jesus said to him, "They have no wine."

   In areas of outer spiritual dryness or in those places in myself where I am conscious of what I lack, how can I open myself, like Mary, to hope and faith and God's providence through Christ?

4. And Jesus said to her, "O woman, what have you to do with me? My hour has not yet come."

   Do I draw back sometimes from letting my own full glory shine? Am I truly humble, or simply fearful and anxious?

5. His mother said to the servants, "Do whatever he tells you."

   What is the Lord telling me to do? And how prompt am I in following through?

6. Now six stone jars were standing there, for the Jewish rites of purification, each holding twenty or thirty gallons.

   What are the untapped areas of abundance in my life and soul? How might the Blessed Mother aid me in discovering and using them more fully to God's glory?

7. Jesus said to them, "Fill the jars with water." And they filled them to the brim. He said to them, "Now draw some out, and take it to the steward of the feast." So they took it and the steward of the feast tasted the water now become wine, and did not know where it came from.

   When was the last time I was surprised and delighted by the wonder of God's action in the world?

8. The steward of the feast called the bridegroom and said to him, "Every man serves the good wine first; and when men have drunk freely, then the poor wine, but you have kept the good wine until now."

   Where do I feel my thirst for God being amply provided for? Church? Home? Family? Friends? Work?

9. This, the first of his signs, Jesus did at Cana in Galilee, and manifested his glory, and his disciples believed in him.

   When was the first time I can remember really seeing the beauty and wonder of the Lord?

10. After this he went down to Capernaum with his mother and his brothers and his disciples, and there they stayed for a few days. The passover of the Jews was at hand.

What are the needs of my own family, spouse, children, siblings in the coming days or week?

Third Mystery: Jesus Proclaims the Kingdom of God's Mercy

1. "Now after John was arrested, Jesus came into Galilee, preaching the Gospel of God, and saying the time is fulfilled, and the kingdom of God is at hand; repent and believe in the Gospel." (Mark 1:14-15)

In what situations – individual, national, or international – do I see the reign of God, the good news of Jesus Christ's message of love and mercy, coming into its fullness?

2. And they came, bringing to him a paralytic carried by four men. And when they could not get near him because of the crowd, they removed the roof above him, and when they had made an opening, they let down the pallet on which the paralytic lay. And when Jesus saw their faith, he said to the paralytic, "My son, your sins are forgiven." (Mark 2:3-5)

Who do I know who has been healed by my forgiveness? From whom do I seek forgiveness, so that I might be reconciled and made whole?

3. Now some of the scribes were sitting there, questioning in their hearts, "Why does this man speak thus? It is blasphemy! Who can forgive sins but God alone?" And immediately Jesus, perceiving in his spirit that they thus questioned within themselves, said to them, "Why do you question thus in your hearts?" (Mark 2:6-8)

Where may my own self-righteousness, my own sense of knowing-it-all, blind me to the creativity of God at work in the world?

4. "But that you may know the Son of man has authority on earth to forgive sins"—he said to the paralytic—"I say to you, rise, take up your pallet and go home." And he rose, and immediately took up the pallet and went out before them all. (Mark 2:10–12)

   What does my pallet consist of? What weaknesses of my own am I comfortable with? What crutches do I continue to lean upon? Where might my faith be strengthened?

5. So that they were all amazed and glorified God, saying "We never saw anything like this!" (Mark 2:13)

   When was the last time I was truly amazed? What can I envision that would truly amaze me?

6. And behold a woman of the city, who was a sinner, when she learned that he was at table in the Pharisee's house, brought an alabaster flask of ointment, and standing behind him at his feet weeping, she began to wet his feet with her tears...and anointed them with the ointment. (Luke 7:37–38)

   Am I uncomfortable with being selflessly served? Are there people to whom it is difficult for me to celebrate or generously give to?

7. Now when the Pharisee who had invited him saw it, he said to himself, "If this man were a prophet, we would have known who and what sort of woman this is who is touching him, for she is a sinner." (Luke 7:39)

   In the past week, whom have I judged to be unworthy, sinful, deserving of reproof or condemnation?

8. And Jesus answering said to him..."Do you see this woman? I entered your house, you gave me no water for my feet...you gave me no kiss...You did not anoint my head with oil, but she has anointed my feet with oil. Therefore I tell you, her sins, which are many, are forgiven, for she loved much." (Luke 7:40, 44-47)

If Jesus said this to me, "Your sins, which are many, are forgiven, for you loved much," would I believe him?

9. And he said to the woman, "Your faith has saved you; go in peace." (Luke 7:50)

On whom do I wish the peace of God today?

10. Jesus said to them again, "Peace be with you. As the Father has sent me, so I send you." And when he had said this, he breathed on them, and said to them, "Receive the Holy Spirit. If you forgive the sins of any, they are forgiven; if you retain the sins of any, they are retained." (John 20:21-23)

What is my relationship to the Sacrament of Reconciliation? Fruitful or fearful? Soothing or painful? How might the Holy Spirit help me use this sacrament to my fuller spiritual benefit?

Fourth Mystery: The Transfiguration (Luke 9:28-37, 43)

1. He took with him Peter and John and James, and went up on the mountain to pray.

As I draw away from the world for these few moments with the rosary, how do I experience the silence?

2. And he was praying, the appearance of his countenance was altered and his raiment became dazzling white.

When has God come to me in a way I did not expect and at first did not recognize?

3. And behold, two men talked with him, Moses and Elijah, who appeared in glory and spoke of his departure which he was to accomplish at Jerusalem.

Are there times or places in my life and ministry where I need God's support, Mary's intercession, or Jesus' inspiration to carry out my own prophetic call?

4. Now Peter and those who were with him were heavy with sleep, and when they wakened they saw his glory and the two men who stood with him.

When was the last time I felt my sleepy soul woken up by surprise?

5. And as the men were parting from him, Peter said to Jesus, "Master, it is well that we are here; let us make three booths, one for you and one for Moses and one for Elijah"—not knowing what he said.

If I let my busyness go, what do I think might happen to me?

6. As he said this, a cloud came and overshadowed them; and they were afraid as they entered the cloud.

When have I entered into the mysteriousness of God's presence, the cloud of unknowing, and how did I receive this grace?

7. And a voice came out of the cloud saying, "This is my Son, my Chosen; listen to him!"

Do I believe God has chosen me to accomplish his will on earth? What has made me believe that—or not?

8. And when the voice had spoken, Jesus was found alone.

Where do I need guidance in following my own special spiritual path?

9. And they kept silence and told no one in those days anything of what they had seen.

   What are the things I still need to keep to myself and ponder within my heart?

10. On the next day, when they had come down from the mountain, a great crowd met him...and all were astonished at the majesty of God.

    On what mountaintop do I seek refreshment for the demands of my daily life?

Fifth Mystery: The Institution of the Eucharist at the Last Supper

1. When Jesus had finished all these sayings, he said to his disciples, "You know that after two days the passover is coming, and the Son of man will be delivered up to be crucified." Jesus knew that his hour had come to depart out of this world to the Father; having loved his own who were in the world, he loved them to the end. (Matt. 26:1-2; John 13:1)

   Where do I anticipate crucifixion in my life — opposition, ridicule, inability to effect change, defeat or loss — and might a greater awareness of God's love help me?

2. Now when Jesus was at Bethany, in the house of Simon the leper, a woman came up to him with an alabaster flask of very expensive ointment and she poured it on his head. But when the disciples say it, they were indignant....But Jesus, aware of this, said to them, "Why do you trouble the woman? For she had done a beautiful thing to me....In pouring this ointment on my body she had done it to prepare me for burial." (Matt. 26:6-12)

How is the Lord preparing me to endure difficulties or grief? What is the passover am I anticipating?

3. Then came the day of Unleavened Bread, on which the passover lamb had to be sacrificed. So Jesus sent Peter and John, saying, "Go and prepare the passover for us, that we might eat it." A man carrying a jar of water will meet you, follow him into the house...and he will show you a large upper room furnished; there make ready. (Luke 22:7-12)

Do I make enough of a place for Christ in my awareness and in my life? How willing and able am I to "make ready"?

4. And when the hour came, he sat at table and the apostles with him. And he said to them, "I have earnestly desired to eat this passover with you before I suffer, for I tell you I shall not eat it until it is fulfilled in the kingdom of God." (Luke 22:14-16)

At what times and in what places do I sense God's desire for me and my companionship most strongly?

5. Now as they were eating, Jesus took bread, and blessed and broke it, and gave it to the disciples and said, "Take, eat; this is my body." (Matt. 26:26)

When in the past has the Eucharist really entered into my soul most powerfully and left an indelible mark on who am I?

6. And he took a cup, and when he had given thanks, he gave it to them, saying, "Drink of it, all of you; for this is my blood of the covenant, which is poured out for many for the forgiveness of sins." (Matt. 26:27-28)

For whom might I receive a cup of blessing today?

7. "Truly I say to you, I shall not drink again of the fruit of the vine until that day when I drink it new in the kingdom of God." (Mark 14:25)

   How is the kingdom of God a reality in my life, in my church, in my community, in my family?

8. And as they were at table eating, Jesus said, "Truly, I say to you, one of you will betray me, one who is eating with me." They began to be sorrowful, and to say to him one after another, "Is it I?" (Mark 14:18–19)

   When have I been betrayed? Whom I have betrayed? And why?

9. A dispute also arose among them, which of them was to be regarded as the greatest. And he said to them, "Let the greatest among you become as the youngest, and the leader as one who serves. For which is the greater, one who sits at table or one who serves? Is it not the one who sits at table? But I am among you as one who serves. (Luke 22:24–27)

   In what ways might Christ or the Blessed Mother tame my own self-seeking, my own ambitiousness, my own need for attention?

10. "You are those who have continued with me in my trials, and I assign to you, as my father assigned to me, a kingdom, that you may eat and drink at my table in my kingdom..." (Luke 22:28–30)

    What images come to my mind when I think of being in God's presence? How do I imagine the eternal feast promised here?

Endnotes

All quotations from Scripture in this text use the Revised Standard Version, Catholic Edition (San Francisco: Ignatius Press, 1966).

Page

46-47   Howard Secher: *www.ourroserosary.com/lazo.htm;*
         Wedding Details, Lore and Tradition:
         www.weddingdetails.com/lore/mexican.cfm.

49-50   Caryll Houselander, *The Mother of Christ* (London:
         Sheed and Ward, 1980), 18-20.

61   Houselander, *The Mother of Christ,* 20.

63   Houselander, *The Mother of Christ,* 21.

95-96   Mary Gordon, *Seeing through Places: Reflections
         on Geography and Identity,* chapter 1, "My Grand-
         mother's House" (web published).

96-97   Helena Sheehan, "Portrait of a Marxist as a Young
         Nun," *www.comms.dcu.ie/sheehanh/portrait.htm.*

125-26   Garry Wills, *Why I Am a Catholic* (New York:
         Houghton Mifflin, 2002), 25-26.

139-40   Linda Michalski and the Holy Bandits, *Sacred Stones
         along the Way* (Chatham, N.J.: Bayley-Ellard High
         School, 2001).

162-63   Christopher Bamford, "Telling the Rosary," *Parabola*
         (Spring 2001): 16-17.

163-64   John Paul II, Apostolic Letter *Rosarium Virginis Mariae,* October 16, 2002.

177-78   St. Augustine, *Letter to Proba.*

184-85   John Paul II, Letter to Artists, April 4, 1999.

188   Gregory of Tours, *De gloria beatorum martyrum,* earliest known Western reference to the Assumption of Mary, quoted in Lawrence P. Everett, C.Ss.R., S.T.D., "Mary's Death and Bodily Assumption," *www.petersnet.net/browse/469.htm.*

194   Mark Brumley, "Mary's Assumption: Irrelevant and Irreverent?" published at *www.mscparishes.org,* Missionaries of the Sacred Heart parishes website.

204   Pope Pius XII, *Ad Caeli Reginam,* On the Queenship of Mary, October 11, 1954.

208-10   Scott Hahn, *Hail, Holy Queen* (New York: Doubleday, 2001), 7-9.

Acknowledgments

This book would most certainly have not been possible without the generosity, thoughtfulness, and willingness of the many people who witnessed to their faith in God and their love for the Blessed Mother by sharing their stories of the rosary with me for inclusion here. Long or short, simple or involved, each of their "beads" shines a unique and special light on the Divine. May they each be blessed: Carol Klufts, Catherine Kilduff, Michael Polyé, Elizabeth Smith, Sister Mary of the Holy Spirit, O.P., Sister Mary of the Holy Family, O.P., André Fleury, Rosemary Hoffman, Cristi Ritchey, Gloria Lewis, Kaitlin Petrone, Andrew Zinkgraf, Kathy Ley, Nicole Betz, Peter Millington, Mary Callaghan, Tom Olszewski, Bridget Sweetin, George Nicastro, Dan DiIorgi, Sister Maryann Scofield, R.S.M., Vince Melillo, and all those who wished to remain anonymous.

I owe a profound personal doubt of gratitude to three individuals who have walked with me through an amazing journey that led into my reception into the Roman Catholic Church and beyond. Kathy Carey, Father José Pimentel, O.P., and Father Christopher Renz, O.P., were selfless, wise, supportive, and challenging when they needed to be. Now they can all stop asking me when I'm going to write my rosary book, and start asking me when I'll be writing my next rosary book.

Similarly, my heart, mind, and soul have been nourished in ways I never imagined through the hospitality of St. Albert's Priory in Oakland, California, seminary for the Western Dominican Province. Worship regularly with those in religious formation and you, too, will find yourself formed, reformed, informed and transformed, as I have. The unfailing ebullience of my own parish, Most Holy Redeemer in the Castro neighborhood of San Francisco, California, has been an equal source of rich grace and growth. All proceeds of this book will be given in thanksgiving to those two communities to continue their mission of bringing Christ to the world in all his magnificence and inclusivity.

The editorial staff of The Crossroad Publishing Company deserves acknowledgment for their expertise, faith, and sensitivity throughout, especially Roy Carlisle. Making a contemplative vision a material reality is no small feat, and I feel so grateful to have had this book birthed so supportively by him. Dorian Gossey's work as copy editor was, similarly, a blessing.

And finally, as always, I thank my family and friends for their support, love, care, and affection over many years and many books, especially Paul.

About the Author

Robert H. Hopcke is a licensed Marriage, Family, and Child Counselor in private practice in Berkeley, California, and is currently the Director of the Center of Symbolic Studies, a non-profit organization he founded with others to further the study of psychology, sociology, and religion. He is well known within the field of Jungian psychology for his numerous books, articles, reviews, and translations published over the past fifteen years, and his national best-seller, *There Are No Accidents: Synchronicity and the Stories of Our Lives,* has been translated into over a dozen languages. His *Guided Tour to the Collected Works of C. G. Jung* has become a standard introduction to Jung's writings in college and universities. He is a frequent guest lecturer across the United States on topics as diverse as the psycho-spiritual dynamics of homophobia, archetypal themes in Italian opera, male psychology, mental health issues in HIV prevention, and the connection between synchronicity and religious experience.

Born and raised in New Jersey, Hopcke attended Georgetown University in Washington, D.C., where he graduated *summa cum laude* with a B.S. in French and Italian. After studying Renaissance art history at the Facoltà di Filosofia e Lettere at the University di Firenze, Florence, Italy, for a year, Hopcke spent a year teaching Italian to artistically gifted, economically disadvantaged students at the Duke Ellington High School for the Performing Arts in Washington, D.C.

Moving to Berkeley, California, in 1980, Hopcke graduated with an M.A.Th. in Pastoral Counseling from Pacific Lutheran Theological Seminary in 1983 and an M.S. in Clinical Counseling from California State University, Hayward, in 1986. He also received advanced training in spiritual direction from the Spiritual Directors Institute at Mercy Center in Burlingame, California. From 1981 to 1989 he was senior intern and then staff supervisor at Unitas Personal Counseling, a low-fee, long-term psychoanalytically oriented clinic associated with the campus ministry of the University of California, Berkeley. He left this position in 1989 to become the coordinator of the AIDS Prevention Program for Operation Concern, the oldest gay and lesbian mental health agency in San Francisco, where he currently serves on the board of New Leaf Services, the successor organization to Operation Concern.

In addition to a small private practice of spiritual direction in Berkeley, Hopcke currently works as a volunteer spiritual director for the Roman Catholic Archdiocese of San Francisco's Detention Ministry Program at the Catholic Chapel of San Quentin. He is co-coordinator of the Peace and Social Justice Group at his own parish, Most Holy Redeemer in San Francisco's Castro District, where he has spent the past few years working with other people of faith to foster greater consciousness and more effective contemplative activism concerning many justice issues, in particular, abolition of the death penalty in California.

OF RELATED INTEREST

Ronald Rolheiser
THE SHATTERED LANTERN
Rediscovering a Felt Presence of God

The way back to a lively faith "is not a question of finding the right answers, but of living a certain way. The existence of God, like the air we breathe, need not be proven." Rolheiser shines new light on the contemplative path of Western Christianity and offers a dynamic way forward.

0-8245-1884-5, $14.95 paperback

Ronald Rolheiser
AGAINST AN INFINITE HORIZON
The Finger of God in our Everyday Lives

"A felicitous blend of scriptural reflection, shrewd psychological observations, and generous portions of letters sent to Rolheiser and his responses." —*Commonweal*

0-8245-1965-5, $16.95 paperback

Henri Nouwen
IN THE NAME OF JESUS
Reflections on Christian Leadership

Featuring new study guide!

Nouwen calls us back to a truly Christian model of leadership, where leaders remember to base their activities in a life of prayer and discernment. Over 150,000 people have read and drawn inspiration from this little gem of Christian leadership. You will too.

0-8245-1259-6, $14.95 paperback

crossroad